The Literacy Coaching Handbook

Learn how to become a more effective literacy coach to ensure lasting changes in teaching and learning at your school. Literacy experts Diana and Betsy Sisson offer clear, research-based strategies that encourage professional development and growth. You'll discover how to . . .

- Understand the various roles that a literacy coach plays, from "change agent" to "data analyst";
- Determine which coaching model to use with your teachers;
- Support your classroom colleagues and raise student achievement;
- Tackle the literacy concerns present in today's schools, and any resistance from classroom teachers who don't want to be coached;
- Design a plan to promote growth centered on assessment and collaboration; and
- Manage the multi-faceted responsibilities of literacy coaching with practical strategies.

Each chapter contains special features such as Coaching Moves and Coaching Questions to help you apply the information to your own situation. In addition, an Appendix offers photocopiable PD tools and study guide questions so you can discuss the ideas with others. With this practical book, you'll have all the guidance you need to overcome challenges and thrive in your coaching role.

Diana Sisson and **Betsy Sisson** are international literacy consultants focusing on professional development and school improvement. They also serve as adjunct professors in the fields of teacher preparation, curriculum and instruction, educational research in literacy, and literacy instruction.

Other Eye On Education
Books Available from Routledge

The Literacy Coaching Handbook

Working with Teachers to Increase Student Achievement

Diana Sisson and Betsy Sisson

Routledge
Taylor & Francis Group

NEW YORK AND LONDON

First published 2017
by Routledge
711 Third Avenue, New York, NY 10017

and by Routledge
2 Park Square, Milton Park, Abingdon, Oxon, OX14 4RN

Routledge is an imprint of the Taylor & Francis Group, an informa business

© 2017 Taylor & Francis

Library of Congress Cataloging in Publication Data
A catalog record for this book has been requested

ISBN: 978-1-138-69259-6 (hbk)
ISBN: 978-1-138-69260-2 (pbk)
ISBN: 978-1-315-53197-7 (ebk)

Typeset in Palatino
by Florence Production Ltd, Stoodleigh, Devon

**To our editor, Lauren Davis,
for all of your support and belief in us**

Contents

Preface

As graduate students seeking reading specialists' certifications, we envisioned careers spent in a reading lab devoted to educating our most vulnerable children. We knew that we would collaborate with our classroom colleagues but that always seemed secondary to our involvement with children. That may have been our expectation, but even after almost 20 years in the field it has never once materialized. Yes, we have worked with students, but since that time so many years ago we have spent the majority of our career coaching teachers.

On one hand, we haven't always had the joy of watching students blossom as they acquire the skills and competencies they need to become engaged, motivated, and self-confident. There is nothing like the feeling that you made the difference in the life of a child. On the other hand, as coaches, we have supported countless teachers to expand their content knowledge, their instructional repertoire, and their own self-efficacy. We aren't always there to see the lasting effects but knowing that you have contributed to the success of even one teacher and the thousands of students whom he or she will teach throughout a single professional career is an extraordinary realization. This is why we believe that coaching is so vital to our schools, our classrooms, and our students. It is awe inspiring to realize that, you, as a coach, can change the lives of children you will never meet!

We have coached in a variety of school settings over the course of our careers in a range of coaching models. We have been peer coaches when we worked in a private school. In public schools we have trained in cognitive coaching, instructional coaching, and, finally, literacy coaching. We have attended workshops, read books and professional journals, "lived" these roles in schools and classrooms, and eventually trained others in their coaching roles.

What have we learned? Coaching is a challenging responsibility, and literacy coaching is the most exacting in which we have ever engaged. It demands that our work with classroom teachers produces significant literacy growth as evidenced by student achievement. Students don't achieve? Then, we are deemed ineffective. In this age of accountability and hyper-awareness of standardized test results, there is no room for error and little time for excuses. This can be an overwhelming burden on literacy coaches.

At times, literacy coaches may work in schools that are ripe for change and embrace innovation as a continuous journey for self-improvement. Their role, however, is not always smooth. They may encounter ambiguity as to what their position entails, anxiety over how to tackle the overwhelming literacy concerns present in today's schools, and resistance from classroom teachers who don't want to be coached. While those outside of this career path sometimes muse that coaches have an easy life, there are innumerable facets of our work that many do not see. It is what lies beneath the surface—what is not seen or what is done out of the spotlight—that can be the most difficult.

When teaching graduate courses for teachers pursuing a reading certification, we task them with locating and interviewing a licensed reading professional and then reflecting on what they have learned and how it informs their own aspirations. Invariably, they report feeling overwhelmed with the scope of responsibilities and content expertise required. Some, unsurprisingly, even suggest that they may finish their degree and stay in the classroom. This is the reality of today's literacy coach. It is demanding, time-intensive, and laden with responsibility. What exactly is a literacy coach? There are innumerable definitions, but we prefer the 2010 description from the International Reading Association (now called the International Literacy Association) when they suggest that those in these roles

> provide coaching and other professional development support that enables teachers to think reflectively about improving student learning and implementing various instructional programs and practices. Often, they provide essential leadership for the school's entire literacy program by helping and creating long-term staff development that supports both the development and implementation of a literacy program over months and years. Such work requires these specialists to work with individuals and groups of teachers (e.g., working with grade-level teams and leading study groups).
>
> (p. 50)

Look at the expansiveness of these responsibilities. Professional development. Improving student learning. Implementing instructional programs and practices. Leadership. School literacy program.

A literacy coach must have an ability to lead, an aptitude to build relationships, a vision for professional development and growth, a command of content, a repertoire of instructional strategies, and the capacity to deliver these goals in a school-wide effort. This is not an undertaking for the faint of heart, the ill-prepared, or the purveyor of the status quo. It is, however, an amazing professional challenge by which you may see your efforts transform those with whom you work—administrators, classroom teachers, and students. With a carefully designed plan for growth based on student data and collaboration and a lot of hard work, you can implement literacy coaching that makes a difference.

In this book, we will identify the realities you will face, guide you to key access points you can leverage for school improvement, and ensure that you sustain your progress to make lasting changes in teaching and learning in your school. It won't be easy, but we can promise you that it will be the most rewarding work you ever undertake!

Introduction

The Literacy Coaching Handbook: Working With Teachers to Increase Student Achievement is our fifth book. In our previous books we have written about literacy practices, instructional techniques, and interventions for struggling readers. This book seems like a natural progression as we turn our attention from teaching students to collaborating with teachers.

We will share how to support classroom colleagues and raise student achievement through three distinct lenses—understanding the power of coaching, the roles a literacy coach assumes, and reflecting on and sustaining change in schools. Within the chapters, we recommend coaching questions to guide instructional improvement (for administrators, classroom teachers, and literacy coaches), additional readings for those who may want to learn more about coaching, and, in the chapters on the roles literacy coaches take on, we highlight coaching moves that elevate coaching practice from good to great! In the Appendices, we have added a Coaching Moves Rating Scale for literacy coaches to track the roles in which they devote the majority of their time as well as to suggest areas that may need more consideration. There is also a list of questions for study and reflection—perfect for individual readers or for book groups in university courses or school systems. So, where do we start?

In Part I, we consider just how important coaching is to teaching and learning. A relatively new innovation in school improvement, we will trace its evolution from its inception in the 1920s and 1930s to its prevalence today in schools across the nation. Along the way, we look at the research and track the influence coaching holds in teacher practice and student achievement. We will also review the major models of coaching to explain what makes each of them unique, what contributions to professional learning they offer, and how they can become a significant component of a literacy coach's professional tool kit.

Part II highlights the roles a literacy coach plays. While it is not possible to discuss everything a coach does in a given day, we emphasize the access points that can leverage the most substantive changes. This is critical because the dizzying array of responsibilities given to a literacy coach may not just be overwhelming but also, and more importantly, may distract from concentrating on the true goal of effecting change. Rather than being weighed down with day-to-day duties, literacy coaches must keep their eyes on the roles that they can take to focus their schools on what Harvard University's Richard Elmore refers to as the "instructional core"—teachers and students in the presence of content.

We begin with the role of *change agent*. The essence of coaching is its intent to generate change. Literacy coaches' entire purpose is to reject the status quo, guiding schools to analyze academic outcomes and to make prescriptive changes to its instructional practices to meet the needs of students. Everything done in schools hinges on this understanding. Literacy coaches' primary emphasis must be one of change. Embrace this fact first, and everything else will come naturally.

In order to make change possible, however, literacy coaches must take on the role of *relationship builder* with those whom they work—both administrators and teachers. If colleagues don't believe in their commitment, their genuine support, and their content expertise, then the effectiveness of coaching will suffer. The literacy coach must make a conscious effort to build bridges so that colleagues see them not as an outside evaluator but as a partner and collaborator striving toward ongoing improvement for students.

Many educators believe that coaching focuses exclusively on instructional practice, but before literacy coaches can engage with instruction they must first be a *data analyst*. Change for the sake of change is meaningless. A plan for change should only be undertaken after a literacy coach and school colleagues have reviewed data (e.g., classroom assessments, standardized high-stakes testing, attendance and behavioral data, and everything in between), examined them for patterns and trends, and reflected how they can inform instruction. Being a data analyst ensures that work is based on evidence and centers efforts on instructional points of improvement.

Once targets for school improvements have been identified, literacy coaches assume the role of a *curriculum expert* to support administrators and teachers in their own practice. Many authorities in coaching argue that being seen as an "expert" is unimportant and may actually be detrimental when working with colleagues. They focus instead on the importance of relation-ships and the need for coaches and teachers to learn together. We strongly disagree with this stance. Think back to the definition of a literacy coach that the International Reading Association released in 2010. It suggested that a coach "enables teachers to think reflectively about improving student learning and implementing various instructional programs and practices." For this to happen, a literacy coach must possess knowledge and expertise. Without it, they serve no purpose. While it is perfectly acceptable, on occasion, to acknowledge that there is something about which they are not certain and that will require them to conduct further investigation, suggesting that literacy coaches know no more about literacy than the classroom teachers they coach is a recipe for disaster. Why come to them for support if their knowledge of literacy is equal to that of the colleagues they coach? Being a curriculum expert is pivotal to change. In this chapter, we will not only make the case for this role but also recommend strategies to support professional learning for literacy coaches to hone their literacy expertise.

For teachers to be successful, they need the resources and materials necessary to sustain their students' learning. The role of *resource provider* may take many forms—locating texts and manipulatives within the school, purchasing key materials, providing lesson planning ideas, etc. Although this is a significant role, literacy coaches must also be cognizant that many teachers will prefer that they maintain this role exclusively. It rarely demands instructional review and can place literacy coaches in the position of a helpful assistant. While providing resources is important, they should not allow themselves to be relegated to only this role. We will show how to transform this relatively innocuous role into deeper reflection and analysis of teacher practice.

Just as literacy coaches should be a curriculum expert, they should also be an *instructional specialist*. Effective literacy coaches work not only with teachers of reading and writing but also with specialists in math, science, social studies, art, music, physical education, etc. If teachers are to ensure that their students can access their texts and their content, then they must be able to utilize powerful instructional strategies to support their learning. Being an instructional specialist brings together all disciplines in an effort to improve teaching practice across the content areas.

Every role has some aspect of professional development, but literacy coaches must also take on the titled role of *professional developer*. In this capacity, they offer a range of learning and growth opportunities (e.g., faculty workshops based on the evidence-based needs of students and teachers, observation and feedback loops, modeling, co-planning, teacher study groups, lesson study, coaching cycles, etc.). All of their work in previous roles should be connected. Rather than disjointed responses to administrator and teacher requests, the roles should be closely linked to one another and to the school's professional development plan. Within this chapter, we will explore different forms for professional development as well as how to network all of these roles into a coherent vision for change.

Part III considers self-reflection of literacy coaches' practice and how to secure coaching goals and their instructional results to be sustainable for future practice. Being a literacy coach requires becoming a school leader, and being an effective leader necessitates the development of a shared vision of what the future can hold. Part III will help literacy coaches transform schools . . . not just for today but for tomorrow.

PART I

How Important Is Coaching for Teaching and Learning?

Coaching can move good teachers to become great teachers. It provides the strongest return on the investment of teaching.

Jim Knight

Teacher quality is the single largest factor affecting student achievement (Carey, 2004; Clotfelter, Ladd, & Vigdor, 2007; Darling-Hammond, 1999; Jordan, Mendro, & Weerasinghe, 1997; Nye, Konstantopoulos, & Hedges, 2004; Perry, 2011); some studies suggest it is the most important (Hightower, Delgado, Lloyd, Wittenstein, Sellers, & Swanson, 2011). Since the late 1990s, researchers have conducted value-added studies in order to delve into student achievement over the course of years to determine if variations, such as teacher effectiveness, have an increasing effect on student performance. Sanders and Rivers (1996) assessed the cumulative effects and determined that students assigned to effective teachers for 3 consecutive academic years scored at percentiles in the 80s. In contrast, when assigned to ineffective teachers for the same 3 consecutive years, student achievement dropped to percentiles in the upper 20s. Considering the policy implications, Bembry, Jordan, Gomez, Anderson, and Mendro (1998) asserted that "it is clear that teachers have large effects on student achievement, that effects have strong additive components over time, and that teacher effects are enough to dwarf effects associated with most other educational interventions" (p. 19).

The inarguable power of educators to influence student outcomes has become a significant rationale for professional development, as it is readily accepted that professional development is the tool by which teachers strengthen their practice. In 2007, Yoon, Duncan, Lee, Scarloss, and Shapley reviewed over 1,300 studies and determined that those teachers who received substantial professional development increased student achievement by 21 percentile points; however, a seminal study by Robert Bush in 1984 determined that attending a workshop and acquiring a description of new teaching practices yielded no more than a 10 percent implementation rate. Adding modeling, practice, and feedback created incremental gains, but implementation soared to an amazing 95 percent when traditional professional learning was paired with coaching.

What's the difference? Noted pioneers in coaching, Beverly Joyce and Bruce Showers (2002) maintain that solidifying a new teaching model into a teacher's instructional practice necessitates 20–25 trials in the classroom over a time of 8–10 weeks. That doesn't happen in a drive-by professional development session . . . it requires the presence of purposeful coaching. They also emphasize five key ways coaching contributes to professional learning and growth.

1. Coached teachers and principals typically practiced the new strategies more and with greater skill than those who received no coaching.
2. Coached teachers used the new strategies with greater skill and more appropriately within the context of their classrooms.
3. Coached teachers demonstrated greater long-term retention of the new strategies.
4. Coached teachers were more apt to explain the new strategies to their students so that students had a greater understanding of the strategies as well.
5. Coached teachers exhibited a greater grasp of the purposes and uses of the new strategies.

Looking specifically at the field of reading and writing, the Literacy Collaborative (2009) studied 17 elementary schools to determine the effects of literacy coaching and found that students' reading performance increased up to 32 percent in 3 years and that the amount of growth could be predicted by the amount of coaching a teacher received. The research confirms an undeniable argument for the power of coaching to influence teaching and learning. Barber and Mourshed (2007) have even made the case that "all top systems, including the rapidly improving ones, recognize that if you want good teachers, you need to have good teachers train them, and this requires focused one-on-one coaching in the classroom" (p. 38).

At the simplest level, coaching is about working collaboratively with teachers to improve instruction and increase student achievement. How those outcomes are actually achieved is based on the coaching model selected and the organizational capacity of the school. In this section, we look back to discover how coaching became established as an effective professional development and the various types of coaching models that exist in today's classrooms.

1

The Evolution of Coaching as a Professional Development Model

The higher you raise the bar of excellence, the more you need coaching.
Robert Hargrove

While coaching as a professional development model is ubiquitous in schools across the United States and is becoming a focal point for change in nations around the world, it is still a relatively new innovation in school improvement. Its roots can be traced to the 1920s and 1930s when reading professionals were first tasked with working directly with teachers and "coaching" them on instructional improvement (Bean, 2009; Toll, 2009). In later decades, however, coaching emerged more systematically and purposefully in reaction to professional development that produced little change in instructional practice or student achievement and continues today as a means for ongoing growth and development.

Coaching Emerges as a Model of Professional Development

The 1950s was a tumultuous period in United States history that gave rise to national movements as diverse as Russia's launch of Sputnik and America's determination to increase the rigor and depth of the country's educational system in order to retain its competitiveness on the world stage alongside the Civil Rights Movement with its desire to right social inequalities in education—both of which deemed professional development a component for school improvement. This focus on professional development continued in the 1960s with the *Elementary and Secondary Schools*

Act of 1965, which included funding for educational trainers. Programming for Head Start, *Title I*, and the *Education for All Handicapped Children Act* enacted in 1975 also included monies for professional development. Despite the use of professional development as a direct support for school improvement in education reform initiatives, there was little change in American classrooms to reflect those efforts.

The failure of professional development to create change in American schools came to light with staff evaluations in the 1970s that suggested as few as 10 percent of professional development attendees actually implemented what they had learned—even when they had volunteered to attend or engaged in extensive training (Joyce & Showers, 1996). In 1980, Beverly Joyce and Bruce Showers conducted a series of seminars, or "coaching sessions," that sought to provide opportunities for teachers to practice the content they had learned—the results were dramatic, prompting them to reason that "modeling, practice under simulated conditions, and practice in the classroom, combined with feedback" (Joyce & Showers 1980, p. 384) offered the most effective professional development design.

The call for coaches grew in the 1980s and the 1990s with the need for literacy coaches—in particular—increasing as literacy become the core of educational reform policy. In deliberating about the limitations of traditional professional development during the 1990s, Lieberman considered the dichotomy of learning between adult and student learners, suggesting that

> it is still widely accepted that staff learning takes place primarily at a series of workshops, at a conference or with the help of a long-term consultant. What everyone appears to want for students—a wide array of learning opportunities that engage students in experiencing, creating, and solving real problems using their own experiences and working with others—is for some reason denied to teachers when they are the learners. In the traditional view of staff development, workshops and conferences conducted outside the school count, but authentic opportunities to learn from and with colleagues inside the school do not.
>
> (1995, p. 67)

The number of reading coaches, however, swelled significantly with the passage of the *No Child Left Behind (NCLB)* legislation in 2001, which provided funding to help support teachers' use of effective reading practices in their classrooms, suggesting that the use of coaches was one avenue for such professional development. Other provisions of *NCLB* created thousands of reading coach positions to staff Reading First K-3 schools.

It has since become accepted, and expected, that coaches present a vital link to assist teachers in changing their practice to support new policy directives (Coburn & Woulfin, 2012). In fact, the educational field has recognized for decades the need of more than a simple one-time workshop for effective professional learning (Darling-Hammond & McLaughlin, 1995; Guskey & Sparks, 1991; Opfer & Pedder, 2011; Showers & Joyce, 1996). Denton, Swanson, and Mathes (2007) affirmed that "there is evidence that professional development with characteristics typical of coaching or mentoring approaches is associated with better outcomes in terms of sustained impact on teacher practice" (2007, p. 570). In studying school reform, however, Elmore (2004) highlighted the difficulties still being experienced in classrooms, arguing that

> the problem [is that] there is almost no opportunity for teachers to engage in continuous and substantial learning about their practice . . . observing and being observed by their colleagues in their own classrooms and classrooms of other teachers in schools confronting similar problems of practice.
>
> (p. 127)

In considering his observations as well as the concerns raised from educators in classrooms across the country, coaching has become a recognized form of professional development and a highly viable conduit for education reform and, yet, it is not consistently utilized or maintained with true fidelity to best practice.

How Coaching Supports Effective Professional Learning

Professional development is typically characterized by an opportunity to increase teacher understanding of content and pedagogy. While it is recognized in many forms (e.g., workshops, seminars, conferences, university coursework), Neufeld and Roper (2003) contend that the key attributes of professional development include the following:

◆ It must be grounded in inquiry, reflection, and experimentation that are participant-driven.

- It must be collaborative, involving a sharing of knowledge among educators and a focus on teachers' communities of practice rather than on individual teachers.
- It must be sustained, ongoing, intensive, and supported by modeling, coaching, and the collective solving of specific problems of practice.
- It must be connected to and derived from teachers' work with their students.
- It must engage teachers in concrete tasks of teaching, assessment, observation, and reflection that illuminate the processes of learning and development.
- It must be connected to other aspects of school change.

(p. 11)

In looking at coaching as a professional development model, it becomes readily apparent that the concept of coaching is embedded in each of these attributes. In fact, this list could easily be mistaken for a job description for a literacy coach!

Additional Readings on the Evolution of Coaching

Bean, R. M. (2015). *The reading specialist: Leadership and coaching for the classroom, school, and community* (3rd ed.). New York, NY: Guilford Press.

Cassidy, J., Garrett, S. D., Maxfield, P., & Patchett, C. (2010). Literacy coaching: Yesterday, today and tomorrow. In J. Cassidy, S. D. Garrett, & M. Sailors (Eds.), *Literacy coaching: Research and practice* (pp. 15–27). Corpus Christi, TX: Center for Educational Development Evaluation and Research.

Hall, B. (2004). Literacy coaches: An evolving role. *Carnegie Reporter, 3*(1), 10–19. Retrieved from www.carnegie.org/reporter/09/literacy/

Moore, D. W., Readence, J. E., & Rickelman, R. J. (1983). An historical exploration of content area reading instruction. *Reading Research Quarterly, 18,* 419–438.

Showers, B., & Joyce, B. (1996). The evolution of peer coaching. *Educational Leadership, 53*(6), 12–16.

2

Models of Coaching

You will never maximize your potential in any area without coaching. It is impossible. You may be good. You may even be better than everyone else. But without outside input you will never be as good as you could be.

Andy Stanley

Coaching has become a familiar form of professional development in today's school systems because professionals in the field recognize that traditional "drive by" trainings can actually decrease teachers' interest in professional growth and increase antagonism to professional learning (Knight, 2000). In contrast, effective coaching that truly makes a difference in the lives of teachers and students relies on an awareness and appreciation of Vygotsky's (1978) Theory of Social Cognitive Development, which asserts that community is central to "making meaning" and that learners internalize new learning after communicating with others—which supports the significance that coaches have in the growth and improvement of teachers' classroom-embedded professional development.

Corresponding to the rise of coaching have come specific coaching models that seek to detail key attributes of effective coaching practice, such as peer, cognitive, instructional, and content coaching. These coaching models serve as a set of guidelines that define the role that a coach plays within an instructional environment as well as a specialized logistical plan for supporting teachers. Despite the uniqueness of coaching models, each of the models shares several key attributes: 1) a defined role of the coach within that model, 2) a focus on supporting teacher growth, 3) an emphasis on instructional planning and reflection, and 4) a commitment to maintain student learning as an indicator of a coach's effectiveness.

Peer Coaching

As early as the 1980s, Joyce and Showers suggested startling statistics that highlighted the powerful results of classroom-embedded coaching in contrast to more traditional forms of professional development.

- ◆ Five percent of learners will transfer a new skill into practice after the study of theory.
- ◆ Ten percent will transfer a new skill into practice after the study of theory and demonstration.
- ◆ Twenty percent will transfer a new skill into practice after the study of theory, demonstration, and practice.
- ◆ Twenty-five percent will transfer a new skill into practice after the study of theory, demonstration, practice, and feedback.
- ◆ Ninety percent will transfer a new skill into practice after the study of theory, demonstration, practice, feedback, and coaching.

In their model, Peer Coaching offers a collaborative, supportive framework for teachers to co-plan, examine instruction, implement new strategies, analyze student work, and observe one another. A coach does not need to have experience or any specific expertise; rather, the coach serves more as a "critical friend" who listens and collaborates as an educator and who may learn as much as the person with whom they are working.

Preferably, teachers volunteer to be participants in Peer Coaching, which has come to encompass an astounding number of professional development platforms, such as co-teaching, co-planning, interdisciplinary unit planning, videotape analysis, looking at student work, book clubs, study groups, curriculum mapping, action research, and so on (National Staff Development Council, n.d.).

Peer Coaching activities, however, can be grouped into two distinct categories: collaborative work and formal coaching. Collaborative work emphasizes the informal efforts taken through mutual learning. It typically has a specific focus, such as instructional strategies, new initiatives, or student learning. Formal coaching embraces a more traditional version of classroom observation, which usually includes an "inviting teacher" requesting support for a particular teaching practice that will come in the form of a three-part cycle of pre-conference, observation, and post-conference. Generally, participants in Peer Coaching initiate their work collaboratively as they build a trusting relationship with one another and then transition to the more formal observation process when they feel comfortable or when the need arises (Robbins, 2015).

In 1996, Showers and Joyce outlined four principles for Peer Coaching:

1. All of the teacher participants must agree to implement the change to be implemented, support one another in this endeavor through collaboration and lesson planning, and gather data on the implementation's effect on students.
2. Participants must not engage in verbal feedback as Showers and Joyce believe that collaborative support with feedback can quickly disintegrate into a more evaluative stance.
3. The paradigm of coaching shifts. The one who is observing does so in order to learn from a colleague and not to provide feedback. The "coach" and "coached" roles can move back and forth fluidly.
4. The collaboration extends beyond observations and conferences to encompass lesson planning, the development of instructional materials, watching one another working with students, and reflecting about how their practices affect student learning.

It should be noted that Peer Coaching has not demonstrated universal success. Some studies have found that peer coaches fail to ask open-ended or probing questions or provide content-specific skills (Busher, 1994; Perkins, 1988). Despite these failings, Peer Coaching is still popular in schools, and it gave the impetus for more rigorous coaching models to surface.

Cognitive Coaching

Developed by Art Costa and Robert Garmston in 1984 and currently used on six continents around the world, Cognitive Coaching focuses on metacognition and independent learning through reflective practice. More specifically, Costa and Garmston (1984/2002) contend that cognitive coaching is unique in that it focuses not only on the outward behaviors of teachers but also on the source of those behaviors. Caine and Caine (1997) echoed this sentiment, asserting that "although actions are important, the thinking that influences and shapes what we do is far more critical" (p. vi). In fact, Ellison and Hayes (2009) argue that it is this concentration on cognitive capacity that makes Cognitive Coaching unique among the models as it exclusively focuses on developing a teacher's skills in engaging with higher intellectual functioning.

Grounded in the clinical supervision work of Robert Goldhammer, Morris Cogan, and Robert Anderson who were working at Harvard's Master of Arts in Teaching program in the 1950s, Goldhammer (1969) and Cogan (1973) rejected the then common practice of supervisors as experts who did all of the talking while teachers listened to instructions of what and how they should change. In its place, they crafted a model in which teachers would be receptive to help from others while still bearing the responsibility of analyzing their own performance and being self-directing.

> Cognitive Coaching is a process during which teachers explore the thinking behind their practices. Each person seems to maintain a cognitive map, only partially conscious. In Cognitive Coaching, questions asked by the coach reveal to the teacher areas of that map that may not be complete or consciously developed. When teachers talk out loud about their thinking, their decisions become clearer to them, and their awareness increases.
> (Garmston, Linder, & Whitaker, 1993, p. 57)

In essence, it embraces three set practices that form a coaching cycle: a planning conference, the observation of a lesson, and a reflection conference. During the planning stage, the coach acts as a mentor who works with the teacher to set goals, strategies, and eventually a self-assessment. Within the classroom, the coach observes, gathers evidence, and makes note of strategies. At the reflection stage, the coach supports the teacher's self-reflection, analyzes the evidence amassed from the lesson, and considers future implications for teaching and learning.

Edwards (2005) compiled a synthesis of research centered on the effects of cognitive coaching and suggested that its documented benefits are extensive, including increases in teacher efficacy, reflection, satisfaction, collaboration, and support as well as improvements in school culture and student achievement.

While this coaching model can have strong implications on teachers' self-reflection and analysis of practice, it does not intentionally address the issue of curricular and instructional knowledge. Thus, participants will become much more metacognitive in their work but may still benefit from support in content area expertise.

Instructional Coaching

Peer Coaching was the first recognized form of classroom-embedded professional development using a collaborative approach, but it was limited by teachers' inability to support one another's professional learning and growth in significant ways. In contrast, Jim Knight from the University of Kansas developed the Instructional Coaching model to support teachers "so that they choose and implement research-based interventions to help students learn more effectively" (Knight, 2006, p. 13).

The theoretic approach behind Knight's (2007) model rests on seven partnership principles that drive the work of reflection of past practice and planning for future practice in the coaching relationship:

1. *Equality*—Coaches and teachers serve as equal partners.
2. *Choice*—Teachers have choice in what and how they learn.
3. *Voice*—Coaches and teachers both have opportunity to share their points of view.
4. *Dialogue*—Coaches and teachers participate in real discussions and arrive at mutually agreed upon decisions.
5. *Reflection*—Coaches provide enough information so that teachers can make their own informed decisions.
6. *Praxis*—Teachers put their work with coaches into practice, recognizing their ability to modify the discussions of coaches to meet their own instructional needs.
7. *Reciprocity*—Coaches expect to learn alongside teachers.

The first step in this model is to determine what instructional strategies will best serve an individual teacher. Knight (2004) suggests that there is a "Big Four" list of teaching practices that have the greatest capacity to affect teacher improvement and should be addressed in a sequential manner: 1) classroom management, 2) content, 3) instruction, and 4) formative assessment. This model posits that if behaviors are out of control in a classroom, then it will be difficult for coaches to work effectively with teachers on their instructional practice. Thus, instructional coaches must first tackle classroom management issues, such as on-task behaviors, classroom expectations, positive teacher feedback, and student interactions. If classroom management is not at issue, then content is evaluated. In essence, does the teacher have a firm grasp of the content and understand the major concepts to be emphasized as well as how to deliver that knowledge to students? If the class is well managed and content delivery is ensured, then the instructional coach considers if the teacher possesses the professional practices to ensure that all students learn. Lastly, the coach assesses if the teacher can draw on formative assessment to inform the teacher as well as the students about how well students are learning content.

Interestingly, Instructional Coaching bases its work on "enrolling" teachers to engage in the coaching process. This can take place though one-on-one interviews, small-group presentations, large-group presentations, informal conversations, and administrative referrals. Once a coaching relationship has been set up, the coach uses five distinct approaches to translate research into instructional practice: clarify what they plan to tell teachers, synthesize the research, chunk it into manageable pieces that correlate to instructional practices, view it through the eyes of teachers and students to determine what it will look like in the classroom, and then simplify it so that there is a common understanding of what it entails.

With the research-based strategies decided, Instructional Coaching centers its work in the classroom with coaches modeling (lessons and instructional strategies), observing (through a co-constructed observation form focused on specific teaching behaviors), and debriefing (both about what the teacher saw the coach do as well as what the coach saw the teacher do). It does not always follow this sequence but is designed to meet the needs of the individual teacher. In any case, the purpose is to support a teacher in mastering a specific teaching practice and then, once mastered, to move on to a new intervention. While this coaching model deepens the concentration on content and instruction, it does not speak directly to the needs of literacy instruction.

Content Coaching

This model focuses on the pedagogy of a particular discipline, such as in literacy or math. Because of its specialized concentration in one content area, such as in literacy, it offers the greatest support to teachers of literacy and content area reading. In the case of literacy coaching, this model proliferated out of the *NCLB* funding that was designed to augment literacy support across the nation's schools.

Content Coaching derives from the work of many educators including Lauren Resnick who developed a set of learning principles that emerged from the theory of incremental intelligence, which suggests that learners can become "smarter" by being aware of who they are as learners and then leveraging that knowledge to implement the appropriate kinds of meta-cognitive strategies and effort. In effect, it argues that educators should emphasize effort over ability. Resnick and Hall (2000) encapsulate this belief in the simple mantra, "smart isn't something you are, it's something you get" (p. 3), and apply this conviction to adult learners as they assert that all teachers, with effort, can become skillful teachers. West and Cameron (2013) carry this idea further, contending that content coaching

> requires expertise that goes beyond "generic" forms of coaching. . . . Therefore content coaches have expertise in at least *two* areas: the content they are helping others teach and how children learn that content. Coaches need this expertise to assess levels of teacher and student understanding and ensure teachers have the expertise needed to give all students access to the concepts embedded in the lesson as well as customize the work with each teacher.
>
> (p. 11)

Cathy Toll, a well-respected author and expert on the subject of literacy coaching, regards it not as an independent model but simply as a category of Instructional Coaching (Toll, 2009). There are elements of Instructional Coaching present, however a line of reasoning exists that literacy coaching extends beyond the "generic" forms of other coaching models as described by West and Cameron (2013) to focus specifically on one particular discipline. Thus, while other models tend to be far-reaching and encompass a broad range of goals and objectives, literacy coaching contents itself with the work of improving student achievement in the area of literacy. This is echoed by the work of Lucy West from the mathematics field, who suggests that

> the goal of content coaching is to cultivate teachers' academic habits of reasoning and discourse associated with their particular discipline and to help them develop a specific skill set that will enable them to cultivate those same habits in their students, habits that will promote student appreciation and understanding of the subject at hand.
>
> (2009, p. 115)

West (2009) also defines the work of Content Coaching through the lens of the "instructional core" and its emphasis on lesson planning, instructional delivery, diagnosis, and improvement of student learning, maintaining that content coaching is not about a particular program or instructional strategy— but about effective instruction as confirmed by student achievement. In essence, this is what differentiates Content Coaching from other models. Coaches in this model are expected not just to act as a supportive collaborator or a reflective questioner, but as an expert source of significant input into classroom instruction. Table 2.1 illustrates the primary characteristics of each

TABLE 2.1 Coaching Model Matrix

	Peer Coaching	Cognitive Coaching	Instructional Coaching	Content Coaching
Keyword	Collaborative	Metacognitive	Pedagogical	Content-Driven
Expert Authority	Bruce Joyce and Beverly Showers	Art Costas and Robert Garmston	Jim Knight	Lauren Resnick Lucy West Cathy A. Toll
Goal	Link between traditional professional development and classroom innovations	Teacher self-direction with capacity for high performance in existing practice	Implementation of research-based instructional strategies	Development of content area skill set that increases educator understanding of discipline as well as how to communicate that understanding to students
Role of Coach	Collegial partner with no verbal feedback	Counselor for autonomous discovery of teacher quality	Specialist of research-based instructional strategies	Expert with significant input regarding specific instructional recommendations tied to student achievement
Knowledge Needed to Implement	No focus on specific instructional strategies or learning theories	Self-reflection and self-actualization	Instructional strategies that are research-based and proven to be effective	Disciplinary expertise; learning theories; instructional strategies
Time Frame for Change	Focus on developing trust and collaborative relationship slows time frame for change	Long-range gains	Change focused on immediate changes in teacher practice	Embraces both short-term "fixes" as well as long-range changes in teaching and learning
Most Suitable	Teachers who are implementing new teaching strategies or curriculum	Teachers who have foundational understanding of teaching and learning but would benefit from reflection	Teachers who may benefit from a range of professional supports	Teachers who may lack content knowledge or classroom experience
Benefits	Nonthreatening; cost effective; strengthens team building	Internal capacity for professional growth	Greater fidelity to research-based instruction	Greater attention to literacy instruction and achievement
Limitations	Little oversight of the coaching process	Results may not be immediately visible	The "Big Four" increases the responsibilities of coaches and dilutes the focus	Requires coaches to have a strong content and instructional knowledge base

of the four coaching models, highlighting their commonalities and their differences.

Each of the coaching models has particular strengths and weaknesses, and none of them is always the "perfect" choice. Rather, coaching models should be differentiated based on staff needs. There is, however, one "right" coaching model for each individual teacher in a particular circumstance. The trick is selecting the one uniquely suited to them.

A strategy to determine the appropriate model or models is by analyzing the instructional core—teachers and students in the presence of content. In analyzing teacher practice, student learning, and content demands, a coach can select a model or combination of models that may be the most effective in strengthening the instructional core and, ultimately, student achievement.

For this to take place, the literacy coach must become knowledgeable about each model and experienced in identifying the model that best matches the needs that exist in any given situation. While all of the coaching models may be used with a range of scenarios, some may be more useful than others. Table 2.2 proposes eight typical situations frequently found in schools. While these are simple scenarios, they are common situations that literacy coaches will encounter in the field.

TABLE 2.2 Coaching Scenarios

What coaching model might be the most useful under these conditions?

1. A teacher who has concerns with student behaviors would benefit the most from Instructional Coaching as this is one of the Big Four focus areas for this model.
2. A teacher unfamiliar with reading content would be helped by Content Coaching in literacy with its emphasis on content knowledge and pedagogy.
3. How about a new teacher? Begin to build a relationship through the collaborative approach of Peer Coaching.
4. Seasoned teachers who have a particular way of accomplishing their instructional goals often grow professionally through the self-reflection, self-analysis, and self-actualization of Cognitive Coaching.
5. Encountering a resistant teacher can be approached through the non-threatening, relationship-building Peer Coaching model.
6. Looking for research-based strategies? Either Content Coaching or Instructional Coaching would be helpful. It depends on the kind of strategies in which the teacher is interested. Instructional Coaching tends to be more generic, while Content Coaching spotlights strategies specific to a content area.
7. Even the best teachers can be challenged with low test scores. Assuming it is an issue that can be addressed instructionally, Content Coaching may be the best response.
8. A dysfunctional grade-level team may benefit from the collaboration inherent in Peer Coaching.

Two cautionary notes should be considered. First, there are nuances in working with colleagues. Just as when teachers search for the underlying needs of students in order to provide targeted support, a literacy coach must carefully review what the real need is of any given teacher before attempting to coach. Second, to incorporate these models, the literacy coach needs to understand them fully and be comfortable utilizing them in daily practice.

This chapter is only an introduction to the most commonly used educational coaching models. It requires effort, time, and continued study to embed these practices into the coaching process, but the result is coming to a school armed with a plan that is prescriptive to the needs of individual teachers and focused on a specific outcome.

Additional Readings on Coaching Models

Costa, A. L., & Garmston, R. J. (2002). *Cognitive coaching: A foundation for renaissance schools* (2nd ed.). Norwood, MA: Christopher-Gordon.

Knight, J. (2007). *Instructional coaching: A partnership approach to improving instruction.* Thousand Oaks, CA: Corwin.

Knight, J. (Ed.). (2009). *Coaching: Approaches and perspectives.* Thousand Oaks, CA: Corwin.

Robbins, P. (2015). *Peer coaching to enrich professional practice, school culture, and student learning.* Alexandria, VA: ASCD.

Toll, C. A. (2014). *The literacy coach's survival guide: Essential questions and practical answers.* Newark, DE: International Reading Association.

PART II

What Roles Does a Literacy Coach Play?

At a recent conference, I overheard a newly hired reading coach lamenting to a colleague, "I just want someone to tell me, what am I supposed to do all day?" Her question is a critical one for reading coaches. How should they spend their time? What are the most important things that coaches should be doing?

Janice A. Dole and Rebecca Donaldson

Literacy coaches have the potential to change the lives of thousands of students who come through the doors of any given school. For that to be true, however, the literacy coach must understand the intricacies of coaching and the distinct roles that highly effective coaches take. These roles directly influence teacher perceptions of literacy coaches and beliefs in their ability to bring about instructional change (Marsh, McCombs, & Martorell, 2012).

Of concern, however, is that literacy coaches in the field report a multitude of issues, such as poorly defined job descriptions (Deussen, Coskie, Robinson, & Autio, 2007), inadequate training and support (Hasbrouck & Denton, 2005), and—most concerning—a lack of focus on coaching itself (Killion, 2009). They point to a never-ending catalog of responsibilities that distract them from working with teachers, including substituting, serving as lunch duty monitor, attending meetings unrelated to literacy, overseeing assessments, working directly with students, and completing paperwork— with over 40 different "roles" identified in recent journal articles and books focusing on literacy coaching (Wren, 2005). This lack of focus can create serious issues in both the perceived and real professional value of literacy coaches in schools as they often find themselves immersed in roles that have little impact on instructional practice (Killion, 2009). Collectively, researchers have documented that coaches spend up to 30 percent of their time on administrative tasks but 10 percent or less time devoted to the work of coaching teachers (Bean, Turner, Draper, Heisey, & Zigmond, 2008; Fullan & Knight, 2011; Knight, 2009a; Marsh, McCombs, & Naftel, 2008; Walpole & Blamey, 2008).

The responsibilities assigned to a literacy coach may not only be steeped in surface routines that hinder working with teachers but also can actually circumvent the crucial goal of making positive strides in teaching and learning. These extraneous tasks have the power to undermine the purpose of coaching—until efforts become fragmented and ineffective. In contrast, Killion (2009) underscores that coaches are

> primarily school-based professional development specialists who work with individuals and teams to design and facilitate appropriate learning experiences, provide feedback and support, and assist with implementation challenges. Their work centers on refining and honing teaching, and their indicator of success is student achievement.
>
> (p. 9)

This is who a literacy coach is in schools. This is the work for which coaches are ultimately responsible and accountable.

This section will delve into the fundamental roles enmeshed in literacy coaching. There is no question that coaching encompasses a wide array of responsibilities, but it is imperative to concentrate efforts in those tasks that constitute effective practices and directly support teacher growth and student achievement. To facilitate these endeavors, there is a "driving question" for each of the key roles that a literacy coach assumes. These questions are designed to illustrate how each role fulfills a different aspect of coaching—each one unique—yet working in tandem with all of the others to consolidate high-quality, powerful coaching support. Each role also highlights a list of coaching moves that are characteristic of the efforts taken within that role.

Beginning with the role of Change Agent, literacy coaches must hold a conviction in their ability to shape improvements in teaching and learning and view their work through the lens of how their actions will propel positive changes in student learning outcomes. There is also a vital need to act as a Relationship Builder among teachers and administrators if a unified literacy team with a common vision is to be fostered. With this groundwork for school-wide change in place, the customization of coaching can be set in motion with the roles of Data Analyst, Curriculum Expert, Resource Manager, Instructional Specialist, and Professional Developer. While each role is inarguably unique and valuable in its own right, the roles also must be connected to develop an organized, cohesive plan for school improvement that looks not just at the whole of the school but at the individual classroom level and the needs of students and their teachers. Literacy coaching is truly multi-dimensional. The trick is to understand what each role entails, what driving question it answers in supporting school improvement, and how the roles fit together like pieces of a puzzle to create an intentional, focused approach to coaching (see Figure P2.1).

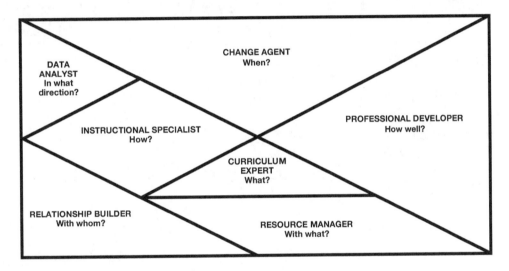

FIGURE P2.1 Literacy Coach Puzzle

Change Agent
DRIVING QUESTION: When?

Literacy coaches are in the change business . . . with coaching comes the sense that something should change.

Cathy Toll

Literacy coaching is not about maintaining status quo. It is not about helping teachers continue the same, safe practices they have always employed. The intent of literacy coaching is change. Change in pedagogical approaches. Change in instructional methods and techniques. Change in how problems are solved. As Cathy Toll (2014) points out, literacy coaches are in the business of change. Some experts argue that there is an option—being a content coach or a change coach—as if the two are mutually exclusive. This belief can gravely undermine a literacy coach's effectiveness.

If literacy coaches do not recognize their role as change agents in schools and imbue this belief in everything that they do, they will find themselves embroiled in surface-level tasks that distract them from their collaboration with teachers and their drive to improve student performance. The thread that runs throughout all that they do as a literacy coach is the unrelenting push toward change—toward transforming school culture into a learning community of teachers actively seeking out ways to strengthen their practice and provide the highest quality instruction for their students.

The driving question for the role as a change agent is—when? The answer is that literacy coaches much recognize their role as change agents begins when they become a literacy coach and permeates every task they undertake . . . with every teacher with whom they work . . . every

COACHING MOVES

- ◆ Collaborate with administrators to define a vision for school improvement.
- ◆ Work with administrators to set focused, prescriptive professional development goals to plan for school improvement.
- ◆ View all responsibilities and tasks through the lens of a change agent.
- ◆ Maintain solution-driven focus.
- ◆ Lead inquiry into best practices.
- ◆ Collaborate with all teachers; don't become a "fixer" of underperforming teachers.
- ◆ Model evidence-based teaching.
- ◆ Advocate for student learning.
- ◆ Facilitate continuous improvement.
- ◆ Be patient but persistent.

day. Literacy coaches embody change, and their focus can never waver from that goal.

How Is a Literacy Coach a Change Agent?

Puig and Froelich (2007) emphasize this role, defining a coach as one who helps teachers to understand not only critical pedagogy at a deeper level but also the need for evidence-based change. To be such a catalyst, literacy coaches must observe current practices, probe into these practices as to their rationale and outcomes, engage teachers in self-reflection, and collaborate on strategies for improvement. This can be difficult as it compels teachers to alter the status quo but, if done, has the potential to produce higher quality implementation of reform practices (Darling-Hammond, Wei, Andree, Richardson, & Orphanos, 2009). Fullan and Knight (2011) actually make the case that

> school improvement will fail if the work of coaches remains at the one-to-one level. Coaches are systems leaders. They need development as change agents at both the instructional level and the level of organizational and system change. It's time to recast their role as integral to whole-system reform.
>
> (p. 53)

Coaches, however, cannot do it alone; they must work hand-in-hand with the administrator in a partnership relationship (Knight, 2005). This is evident as

> no matter how much a coach knows, and no matter how effective a coach is, the principal's voice is ultimately the voice most important to teachers. For that reason, coaches must understand fully their principal's vision for school improvement, and principals need to understand fully the interventions that their coach has to offer teachers.
>
> (Knight, 2009a, p. 52)

So how administrators view the goal of coaching has indelible influence in the way in which literacy coaches fulfill their tasks and how effective they are in their position. Administrators set the parameters by which coaches function in a school through their power to safeguard coaching responsibilities that preserve their attention on teaching and learning, to create schedules that allow for coaches and teachers to meet both individually and in teams, to provide time to analyze data as a means to inform both coaching and classroom instruction, to confer themselves on a regularly agreed-upon time to review the effects of coaching on instructional improvement, and, most importantly, to communicate to teachers the value of coaching in the school.

Literacy coaches can only be change agents with the endorsement of administrators. They cannot assume this role without the credible source of authority held by administrators. A lack of focus from the true purpose of coaching and the corresponding discontent experienced when they feel like they are not making a difference is one of the most common complaints of literacy coaches. Literacy coaches must take the stance to administrators that their intention is to be a change agent, to work collaboratively with their colleagues to improve teaching and learning—and ultimately, student achievement. As literacy coaches continue to define their role, they must also be cognizant that their ability to bring about change additionally rests on whom administrators direct them to coach.

What Teachers Are the Focus for Change?

Coaches are often asked by administrators to "fix" teachers who are perceived as low performing. That, however, can be a significant misstep. While teachers who struggle cannot be ignored, neither can they be the only focus. Making weak teachers a priority negates efforts to increase school-wide change and perpetuates the myth that coaches don't work with "strong" teachers. An effective coach can, should, and must collaborate with all teachers. Knight (2004) maintains that coaching can transform good teachers into great teachers, and Saphier and West (2009/2010) even argue that it is with the strongest teachers where coaches should begin their efforts. These teachers can then become "lead teachers" whom others can observe and learn from in authentic classroom settings.

Change efforts, however, can be hindered by resistant teachers. Working with teachers who are unwilling to collaborate is a prevalent issue that literacy coaches raise. How do you engage a teacher who doesn't want your help? It can be challenging, and often times, discouraging. While building relationships (See Chapter 4) is an essential aspect of diminishing resistance, Jim Knight (2009b) also recommends that opposition can be countered through eight practices that concentrate on providing structured support of evidence-based instructional practices with ongoing monitoring of the effectiveness of their implementation.

1. Implement proven teaching practices that have a positive bearing on achievement.
2. Utilize data to monitor the effect of these practices.
3. Offer quality coaching to ensure that teachers see the practices in action and their results in the classroom.
4. Provide clear explanations of the practices but leave opportunities for teachers to implement them in ways according to their own pedagogical approach and the needs of their students.
5. Encourage teachers to voice their choices and then value those choices.
6. Narrow professional development down to focused practices.
7. Align professional work to these specific practices.
8. Increase relational trust.

These suggestions offer a clear plan for addressing most resistant teachers, but what about those who continue to rebuff collaborating with a coach? Most experts recommend working with those who "want" a coach in their rooms and wait for resistant teachers to come later after they see the benefits of the coaching relationship. This will certainly alleviate any discord that may be present, but it also weakens a literacy coach's ability to stimulate school-wide change, relegating collaboration to pockets of a school. While coaches must maintain collegial, respectful relationships with their colleagues, the effect of not working with less readily enthusiastic teachers adds to the perception that coaching is just for some, and the focus is on teachers and not student achievement. It is, in fact, student achievement that provides an entry point into classrooms. Analyzing student data in an objective manner with grade-level or content area teams re-directs the spotlight away from teachers and toward looking at instruction as the vehicle to improve student learning. It is not personal. It is not subjective. It certainly is not evaluative. It is, however, the aim for all teachers—those who welcome coaches and those who may be resistant.

How Does Change Happen?

What makes a literacy coach unique in a school setting is the way in which the coach is positioned to see the big picture—the needs of students, the instructional practices of teachers, and the expectations of administrators (see Figure 3.1). The value of this viewpoint is predicated on the coach's ability to help others see that same picture and understand what part they play in the system as a whole, breaking down the culture of isolation that often pervades schools. Sustainable change happens when all of the stakeholders are engaged and involved in the reform process. This interdependence is facilitated by and strengthened through the literacy coach.

What's more, "for meaningful change to occur, teachers must have a voice in the process of their own learning. Therefore, coaches must heed teachers' voices so that coaching is differentiated relevant to the concerns and interests of their teachers" (Stover, Kissel, Haag, & Shoniker, 2011, p. 499). Just as expert instruction attends to the unique needs of students, adept coaching demands a tailored approach, a personalized support level, a specific instructional focus, and one-on-one interactions with teachers to address the needs that they have. Coaching is not a uniform approach—but rather is in a perpetual state of revising and adapting to adjust to individual teachers and their needs.

Ultimately, however, change will not happen without an unswerving belief that change is at the heart of coaching. It is literacy coaches' task to keep that visible in every conversation and in every coaching move they make—be it through the daily work of instructional planning and teaching to the yearly plan of school improvement and professional development. Change must be embedded in every facet of coaching.

Literacy coaches are change agents. It is that simple and that immense. Change is the fundamental goal all literacy coaches uphold. They strive to transform schools into professional learning cultures who actively seek out

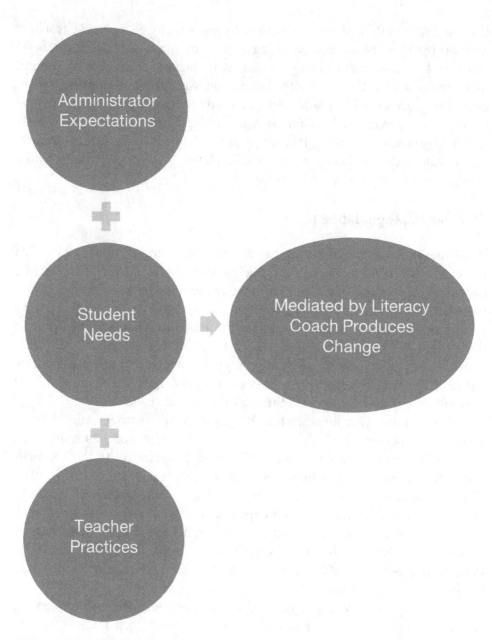

FIGURE 3.1 How Change Happens

ways to improve their practice and ensure that students succeed. Being a change agent is not easy, nor is it accomplished quickly, but it does drive the work that coaches do and offer real hope for improving the learning outcomes of students.

? COACHING QUESTIONS

1. What does the data reveal to us about student needs and ways in which we might need to adjust our instructional approach to improve teaching and learning? (for Administrators and Teachers)
2. What is the change that you want to see in the literacy program? (for Administrators)
3. How can I help you meet, and hopefully exceed, the expectations that the principal(s) holds for the literacy program? (for Teachers)

Additional Readings on Being a Change Agent

Blachowicz, C. L. Z., Obrochta, C., & Fogelberg, E. (2005). Literacy coaching for change. *Educational Leadership*, *62*(6), 55–58.

Fullan, M., & Knight, J. (2011). Coaches as system leaders. *Educational Leadership*, *69*(2), 50–53.

Saphier, J., & West, L. (2009/2010). How coaches can maximize student learning. *Phi Delta Kappan*, *91*(4), 46–50.

Steckel, B. (2009). Fulfilling the promises of literacy coaches in urban schools. What does it take to make an impact? *The Reading Teacher*, *63*(1), 14–23.

Sturtevant, E. G. (2003). The literacy coach: A key to improving teaching and learning in secondary schools. Alliance for Excellent Education. Available at http://all4ed.org/

4

Relationship Builder

DRIVING QUESTION: With Whom?

The core of professional development is the trusting relationship between teacher and coach. When this relationship is fostered, literacy coaches come to know, understand, and appreciate the teachers' level of experience, expertise, and interests. Because of this knowledge, the coach can more effectively support them in their professional growth.

Katie Stover, Brian Kissel, Karen Haag, and Rebecca Shoniker

Relationships. Without them, it can prove nearly insurmountable to institute change in a school. Relationships open the doors to collaboration, to a willingness to be innovative, and an acceptance both to give and to take feedback as a means for professional growth. While the first role literacy coaches assume is that of change agent, without the role of relationship builder, instructional improvement is limited.

Relationship builder is the only role that has no direct link to content. It is not about pedagogical knowledge, instructional capability, or an understanding of organizational change efforts; this is about people. While it may seem unwarranted to include this as a key aspect of coaching, relationship building is essential (Matsumura, Garnier, & Resnick, 2010; Neumerski, 2013). It has the capacity either to transform professional school culture or to undermine efforts—regardless of a literacy coach's content area capabilities or expertise with classroom instruction.

♟ **COACHING MOVES**

- ◆ Foster a safe environment.
- ◆ Develop collegial relationships.
- ◆ Listen.
- ◆ Maintain confidentiality.
- ◆ Follow through on requests.
- ◆ Seek out teachers for professional dialogue.
- ◆ Understand that coaching is not a top-down model.
- ◆ Set clear expectations for work between the coach and the classroom teacher.
- ◆ Link coaching model to the needs of individual teachers.
- ◆ End the misconception that coaching operates as a deficit model for only those teachers who need to be "fixed."
- ◆ Welcome teachers' initiation of coaching support.
- ◆ Support teacher experimentation with new practices.
- ◆ Ask open-ended questions to spur deeper thinking.
- ◆ Encourage self-reflection of professional practices.

How Important Is It to Build Relationships with Administrators?

The driving question for this role is "with whom"—with whom do coaches work and, thus, with whom must they build relationships to ensure strong collaboration? While the most obvious answer is the relationship formed between themselves and the classroom teachers with whom they work in partnership, the first relationship that coaches must foster is with the building administrator. It is the administrator who plays the most critical role in the ability of the literacy coach to be effective as "to a large extent, the ultimate success or failure of an instructional coaching program can be attributed to the decisions and actions of building-level administrators" (Hanover Research, 2014, p. 13).

Administrators cannot be divorced from the equation of change— principals, teachers, and coaches must act as a team to improve practice. Just how important are they? Instructional leaders, like literacy coaches who are linked with principals who actively support them, exhibit increased effectiveness (Bean, Draper, Hall, Vandermolen, & Zigmond, 2010). In fact, teachers are more willing to work with coaches when they are endorsed by the principal and seen as working collaboratively with them (Matsumura et al., 2010).

The relationship is launched with developing a vision for school improvement. One of the first conversations that literacy coaches must have with building administrators is to determine what goal has been set that encompasses the best of both teaching and learning. This direction for improvement must be articulated and clearly defined, allowing administrators, coaches, and teachers to work toward a common understanding of what they collectively hope to achieve. Without it, everyone's efforts, including those of the literacy coach, will be unfocused and disconnected. Some administrators embody instructional leadership, maintaining a clearly articulated vision for their school that allows them to define the parameters of change as well as to prioritize what needs to be done to be successful in their endeavors. In this case, the coach needs only to confer with the principal and determine how to support the goals already established. If, however, there is no cohesive vision in place, the coach needs to work alongside the principal and teachers to learn what core values exist and identify potential targets for improvement—specifically concentrating on reading achievement and how the literacy program may be adjusted based on the needs of the school—and then how coaching will be integrated into that improvement process. These efforts may center around improving the literacy block, academic rigor, high-quality writing instruction, or any number of other goals and should be grounded in data with implications for student learning outcomes.

Once those plans are finalized, the real work begins. The literacy coach and principal should meet frequently (weekly, if possible) to review the goals in place and how coaching efforts are supporting these efforts. This close relationship and ongoing collaboration lessen the potential for assigning roles and responsibilities that detract from improvement efforts and ensure a consistent approach with a greater likelihood of sustainable change. With a clear, concise direction for moving forward, the literacy coach must begin to build teacher relationships.

? COACHING QUESTIONS

1. What vision do you have for the school literacy program? (for Administrators and Teachers)
2. What do you hope teachers and students will achieve? (for Administrators)
3. How can I help improve student learning? (for Administrators and Teachers)

Why Are Relationships with Classroom Teachers So Crucial?

A literacy coach's effectiveness rests in large part on the ability to collaborate on content knowledge and instructional expertise, and this sharing takes place primarily through professional interactions with teachers (Bean & Eisenberg, 2009). Coaching success, then, is predicated on maintaining collegial, trusting relationships with teachers (Buly, Coskie, Robinson, & Egawa, 2006; Denton & Hasbrouck, 2009; Tschannen-Moran & Tschannen-Moran, 2010) as a coach's interpersonal skills are as valuable as the content knowledge for which they were hired (Brown, Reumann-Moore, Hugh, du Plessis, & Christman, 2006). Daly (2012) even makes the argument that "a coach's ability to move information and strategies may be dependent on whether the coach has adequate social ties to diffuse resources throughout a system; absent those relationships, the expertise and knowledge of the coach may remain personal assets" (p. 6).

The importance of this relationship cannot be overstated, nor can it be taken for granted. It forms the bedrock of all coaching models, and it must be recognized that

> the nature of the teacher-coach relationship is delicate. Teachers, who were once isolated within four walls, now find themselves with classroom partners. Coaches, who enter classrooms wanting to make big changes, must do so without evaluation. Trust, which is nurtured over time, forms the foundation for learning . . . and together they discover what needs to happen next in order for students to grow as learners. Eventually, coaches leave the classroom, and teachers navigate these inquiries on their own.
>
> (Stover et al., 2011, p. 499)

There is a long tradition of isolation in school culture in which teachers have planned by themselves, taught by themselves, and reflected by themselves. It necessitates a complete shifting of that paradigm to view teaching not as an isolated activity but as a collective action—one in which administrators, teachers, and coaches hold a shared vision of what the literacy program should look like and accomplish.

Changing this mindset, however, is challenging. Teachers can feel vulnerable and threatened by having another educator in their class. Those feelings are exacerbated if that educator is identified as a literacy coach—someone characteristically deemed as an expert in the field who observes and gives feedback about their teaching performance, suggests unfamiliar practices that may disrupt their typical routine, and obliges them to reflect critically about data, student learning outcomes, and perhaps even the pedagogical approach they have maintained throughout their professional career. Being cognizant of these sensitivities is crucial if the literacy coach is going to be productive and welcomed into teachers' classrooms.

How Do Literacy Coaches Build Relationships with Classroom Teachers?

Forming a professional relationship is launched with personal interactions. A common suggestion found in journal articles and books on coaching is to help teachers in daily tasks, such as photocopying, covering their classes so that they can take a break, or bringing them a cup of coffee when they can't leave their room. While these are certainly kind gestures, they also pose a serious threat to how teachers view the literacy coach. A common complaint about coaches is that they don't have the demanding schedule that classroom teachers have. By volunteering, then, to assist their colleagues a typical byproduct is that they inadvertently reinforce this misconception. Rather than viewing this type of support as a friendly overture, classroom teachers may come to see these actions as confirmation that coaches simply have a less arduous schedule. An alternative to this manner of assistance is to furnish support through an academic avenue, such as offering to co-plan or to prepare a plan of action for a struggling student.

In addition, there are certain "golden" rules that should be followed in order to build and maintain trusting relationships with classroom teachers. These are non-negotiable and must be safeguarded in all interactions. Break a golden rule, and break the trust. This is critical as, once that trust is broken, the resulting fractured relationship can rarely be fully restored.

- ◆ **Listen**. Before literacy coaches can begin to tackle academic concerns, they must first listen—actively listen—to the perspective of the classroom teacher. Rather than rush to solve the problem, they need to set aside time for teachers to give voice to their experiences, their concerns, and their desires for support. Coaching rests on conversations and interactions that act as a framework for instructional improvement efforts.
- ◆ **Maintain confidentiality**. Inviting a colleague into the thought processes behind instructional planning, into the classroom to observe how teaching and learning take place, and into the assessment analysis that drives instruction requires a great deal of trust on

the part of the teacher. That level of professional intimacy cannot be preserved if the content of that partnership is shared with others without the express permission of the teacher. What is shared in one-on-one coaching sessions must remain private to provide a safe environment in which teachers can candidly reflect and grow in their own practice.

◆ **Follow through on requests**. Literacy coaches are approached daily with a myriad of inquiries, such as for additional resources, modeling, co-planning times, and questions about curriculum and instruction. Failing to address these requests and respond dependably can weaken relationships and deteriorate teacher belief in how committed a coach may be in supporting their work. The literacy coach should respond within the day the request was made. If that is not possible, then that delay should be communicated with a later time provided.

◆ **Understand that coaching is not a top-down model**. It should involve the teacher in problem solving about ways to hone teaching and learning. A basic principle in adult learning is the need for teachers to be active in their own learning and involved in the selection of what they learn, how they learn, and how their learning will be assessed. It must also be realistic and pertinent to their work—and just how realistic and pertinent it is will ultimately be determined by the classroom teacher. Without that consensus, little change will take place as adult learners typically reject prescriptive measures in which they have no control or voice.

◆ **Set clear expectations for the work that coaches and teachers will do together**. Ambiguity has no place in the coaching relationship. Conversations, actions, and responsibilities must be explicitly known and understood by both the literacy coach and the classroom teacher. Deviation from the expectations created by the teacher reduces the potential for a strong working partnership.

◆ **Eradicate the misconception that coaching operates as a deficit model**. Literacy coaches do not work solely with those in need of being "fixed" but also embrace those who provide high-quality instruction but would benefit from collaborating with another professional to refine their practice. If coaching is viewed as a tool only to "fix" teachers, it places those teachers working with the literacy coach at a disadvantage and suggests an imbalanced partnership. It should be made public that coaching benefits all teachers through collegial sharing and that the literacy coach partners with all teachers—not just a select few in need of structured support.

In addition to these rules of relationship building, Costa and Garmston (2002) place trust building into three distinct contexts: trust in self, trust between individuals, and trust in the coaching process. Trust in self and trust between individuals are indisputable, but trust in the coaching process itself must not be overlooked. If the relationship between the literacy coach and the classroom teacher is to be successful, the teacher must have faith that their work together will be non-evaluative and will center on instructional improvement for the benefit of students.

Despite the efforts literacy coaches make to build trusting relationships with the classroom teachers with whom they partner, they will encounter those who are not welcoming to their presence or their offer for support. With that reality in place, the next move is to determine how to address this resistance in a positive, productive manner.

In What Ways Can Relationships Be Leveraged to Counter Resistant Teachers?

Robbins (2015) suggests that many literacy coaches are unable to make substantive differences with instructional practice because, although they have significant content knowledge, they have not focused enough on relationship building and developing trust with those whom they coach. That said, coaches often hold a misperception regarding potential receptiveness of their classroom colleagues. It is commonly asserted that those teachers who have been in the field the longest may be the most resistant to change, and those teachers who are characterized as novices are more open to innovations. That idea may prove inaccurate and, ultimately, damaging to coaching. Joyce, Bush, and McKibbin (1982) studied this phenomenon and found no significant relationship between teaching experience and receptivity to participate in professional development but, by 2002, Joyce and Showers related that their experience in the field indicates that advancing age correlates to increasing openness as a learner. What this suggests is that literacy coaches may encounter the most resistance from those new to the classroom with less than 5 years of experience in the profession. When working with them, novice teachers may cling to the instructional theories and practices they learned in their training programs and reject other viewpoints or evolving understanding about teaching and learning.

Joyce and Showers (2002) also discuss particular growth prototypes related to teachers' receptivity to professional development. First, they defined *gourmet omnivores* as teachers who actively sought out learning opportunities and were likely to implement new innovations into their instructional practice. Within this category, 10 percent were highly engaged in learning and growth, and another 10 percent were slightly less active but still exhibited the basic characteristics. These teachers are often overlooked in the coaching process in favor of needier teachers identified as struggling and in need of support. Partnering with highly engaged teachers, however, not only diminishes the belief of coaching as a deficit model as discussed earlier in the chapter but also enhances instructional practices for skilled teachers who may, in turn, serve as models of effective teaching and enthusiastically share their knowledge with others. Conversely, when coaches expend all of their time and energies on under-performing teachers, the coaching process takes on a "triage" mentality in which teachers are identified for support by those in most need. This may seem sensible; however, triage necessitates that those in most need are provided for while others may be unavoidably neglected. A school's literacy program cannot make substantial, sustainable improvement with such a splintered approach.

By far the greatest number of teachers, approximately 70 percent, demonstrated characteristics of the *passive consumer*—generally open but dependent on with whom they are working for whether or not they were active or inactive in implementation. These are the teachers who will attend professional development if required but not seek them out or attempt to incorporate new innovations into their practice without ongoing support. Literacy coaches must be cognizant and develop a plan for how to engage less self-motivated teachers who may escape notice. They may not directly seek out the coach for collaboration; so it is the literacy coach who must make concerted efforts to connect with them through relationship building.

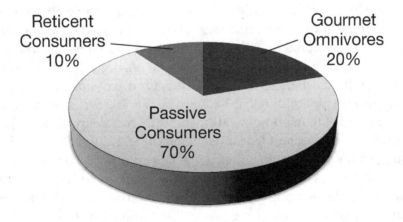

FIGURE 4.1 Teacher Growth Prototypes

The most concerning archetype, however, is the *reticent consumer* who take in 10 percent of teachers. These are colleagues who aggressively push away opportunities for growth, fail to take advantage of professional development opportunities, and are often hostile when compelled to attend. Within the context of coaching, the reticent consumer is one who openly declares, "I don't need coaching" while striving to protect established, comfortable practices and rejecting the unknown and unfamiliar. Unfortunately, these same teachers may be identified as in need of structured support. Of greater concern, often coaches are counseled to stay away from the most resistant teachers and align themselves to those who are openly accepting of working with them. This course of action produces several troubling consequences—teachers who may profit from the coaching process fail to gain its benefits, collaborating with the coach becomes voluntary and based on the preferences of teachers and not the needs of students, and teachers who may have previously found collaborating appealing may come to devalue the coach as unnecessary.

While it should never take on a contentious tone, literacy coaches must address resistant teachers. Possible avenues for facing this issue include meeting one-on-one so that the environment is more informal and less threatening. Focusing on student work and de-emphasizing the teacher also serves to lessen the antagonism as resistant teachers often fear accusations against their professional skills. Another entry point is to concentrate on one specific aspect rather than more global attention so that the work is seen as more manageable and less intimidating. Whatever path to relationship building is taken, it is important to remember that leaving a resistant teacher out of the coaching process weakens the possibility for growth for all teachers.

Relationships—with administrators and teachers—prove vital as coaches begin to initiate tough conversations about data, student achievement, curriculum, instructional practices, and the professional beliefs that propel classroom instructional and assessment. While relationships increase levels of influence with teachers so that these difficult discussions can take place in meaningful ways, building trust cannot be the sole focus so that coaches spend their time developing relationships to the delay and neglect of professional dialogue about teaching and learning. Killion (2009) makes the wise suggestion that "saying that a coach's role is to support teachers misleads teachers. A coach's primary responsibility is to improve student learning" (p. 27). Leveraging the role of relationship builder certainly remains an integral aspect of the coaching process, but it must be remembered that its power is in its ability to augment teaching and learning. With relationships in place, literacy coaches should direct their efforts to data analysis and supporting school improvement efforts.

Additional Readings on Building Relationships

Carr, J. F., Herman, N., & Harris, D. E. (2005). *Creating dynamic schools through mentoring, coaching, and collaboration*. Alexandria, VA: ASCD.

Ippolito, J. (2010). Three ways that literacy coaches balance responsive and directive relationships with teachers. *The Elementary School Journal*, *111*(1), 164–191. doi: 10.1086/653474

Lowenhaupt, R., McKinney, S., & Reeves, T. (2014). Coaching in context: The role of relationships in the work of three literacy coaches. *Professional Development in Education*, *40*(5), 740–757. doi: 10.1080/19415257. 2013.847475

Pletcher, B. (2015). Literacy coaching advice: Cultivating healthy working relationships with teachers. *Texas Journal of Literacy Education*, *3*(1), 50–56.

von Frank, V. (2010). Clarify the coach's role: Solid partnership with principal is key to effectiveness. *The Learning Principal*, *5*(5), 3–7.

5

Data Analyst

DRIVING QUESTION: In What Direction?

Numbers have an important story to tell. They rely on you to give them a clear and convincing voice.

Stephen Few

Look around. Schools are surrounded by mountains of student data with a jaw-dropping number of ways to process everything. Data tracking. Data charts. Data binders. Data analysis. Data-driven decision making. It cannot be escaped. It permeates nearly every conversation about education, but just how valuable is it? Honestly? Teachers are caught in a tidal wave of "data talk" with little to show for their efforts. Unless used reflectively, all of the work around data is simply a distraction from teaching and learning. The reality is that data represent numbers, which by themselves have little effect on instruction. It is how educators analyze data, hypothesize about what the numbers reveal about student learning, and the instructional adjustments put in place that empower school improvement.

In the case of literacy coaching, being a data analyst is the first step when engaging teachers on the subject of instructional improvement and answers the question of "in what direction" by providing clear guidance for enhancing teaching and learning. This may seem contrary to conventional wisdom. Many coaches complain about wearing so many hats that they are constantly running to keep up with the demand. They are working as hard as they possibly can. The question here is: Is all of their work making a difference? Working hard is not the same as working smart. The difference between them is the analysis of data. Without data, how do literacy coaches

COACHING MOVES

◆ Offer demonstrations of assessment administration and scoring to ensure a standardized approach to grading practices.
◆ Collaborate with teachers to analyze and interpret data.
◆ Identify teacher needs based on data.
◆ Support teachers in their ability to use data to drive instruction.
◆ Emphasize a problem-solving lens.
◆ Rely on student data to ground coaching support.
◆ Help teachers adjust instructional strategies based on data and student need.
◆ Guide teachers in their monitoring of student data.

know where to begin? How do they know where to focus their attention and their support, and how do they know if they have been effective?

This is a literacy coach's reality. Data remains at the core of powerful instructional coaching. Data should drive all efforts for ongoing instructional improvement with teachers, serve as a means to make reflective decisions for improving student achievement, and, ultimately, measure the success of their work together. In short, literacy coaches should provide the kind of intensive assistance that ensures that their schools develop a data-driven culture—one in which data are viewed as one of the best tools at their disposal to provide a high-quality education and as a lever for instructional improvement.

Why Is Looking at Data So Critical for Literacy Coaches?

Teachers appreciate having access to student data yet often voice a concern about how to interpret the results, investigate the implications for learning, or craft instructional strategies in response to the results (Cosner, 2012; Means, Chen, DeBarger, & Padilla, 2011; Oláh, Lawrence, & Riggan, 2010). A 2015 study by the Bill and Melinda Gates Foundation found that 78 percent of teachers surveyed believe that data can validate student achievement, with one teacher remarking: "[Examining data in detail] allows me to predict where students are going to get stuck, predict their hiccups, their successes, and their challenges. You have to really know where each student is struggling in order to transform their learning" (p. 25).

Yet 67 percent of those same teachers were dissatisfied with the effectiveness of the data and tools with which they worked in their school systems, reporting that teachers felt that data were siloed, difficult to aggregate, one-dimensional, inflexible, and, most concerning, untrustworthy.

While this discontent with a data-driven culture is common, student data form the basis of literacy coaching. If analyzed through an inquiry lens and utilized as a guide for instructional improvement, data provide a strong entry point into coaching teachers, revealing where the most support is needed and showing what needs to be done to strengthen the instructional core of a classroom. What's more, if data are examined with laser-like focus for no other purpose than to discover improvements in teaching and learning, they will expose the academic health of a school—what's working, what's not, and what assumptions administrators and classroom teachers are holding that may not hold true in the light of hard numbers.

What Types of Data Should Be Examined?

For data to be useful, they must be analyzed within the context in which they were collected and the purpose that they were designed to serve. For example, a high-stakes standardized test will typically provide a benchmark score to indicate the general academic health of students but not an in-depth analysis of exact strengths and weaknesses. So, results may indicate an area of concern but offer no clear view of how to support the teacher or the students.

They should also never be reviewed in silos where data are seen as independent of one another. The strength of data analysis centers on refraining from drawing conclusions from a single data point (i.e., one assessment) and focusing, instead, on triangulating multiple pieces of information in order to develop evidence-based hypotheses about student performance. Thinking back to that standardized test, those results alone will never be sufficient to navigate among the vast array of literacy skills and competencies students must develop to say with any certainty where to initiate instructional improvement.

So, what should be done? Rather than relying on one data point, a better approach is to "triangulate" multiple pieces of data to gather a more precise representation of student performance. One assessment can never reveal the true ability of students, nor can it suggest with unequivocal reliability the strengths and weaknesses of instruction inside of a classroom. Using multiple data points, however, increases insight into the teaching and learning taking place within classrooms, transforming this information into actionable

? COACHING QUESTIONS

(for Administrators and Teachers)

1. What should students know and be able to do?
2. How will we assess student performance?
3. What do demographic, attendance, informal assessment, and behavioral data suggest about student learning?
4. Do any patterns or trends emerge about students, sub-groups, performance levels, or skill areas?
5. Are we making progress in closing achievement gaps? If so, how? If not, what changes in practice should we make?
6. What skill areas need the most reinforcement?
7. How will we address the specific learning needs of all of our students?
8. In what ways can I offer support—professional development, instructional strategies, resources?

knowledge through which hypotheses can be formed as to what can be done to improve learning and what coaching move will support that growth.

Too often, teachers focus their attention on one piece of data—most often the high-stakes testing for which they are held accountable. The task is to collaborate with teachers in looking within the "data warehouse" of a school to glean a clearer understanding of student learning. In most cases, this can be accomplished by looking at three major categories of student data: demographic data, student learning data, and behavioral data. This process takes more time than simply analyzing a single piece of data, but it also encourages a much richer understanding of how students are truly performing as well as what mitigating factors may be influencing their performance. Let's take a look at these different types of data and how they strengthen instructional improvement efforts.

Demographic Data

While often overlooked when considering student performance, demographic data provide insight into students' lives – their home lives as well as their past educational experiences and achievement levels. These data can be accessed through a number of avenues. *Cumulative folders* contain a range of helpful records, including schools students have attended (Has the student remained in one school, or does the record document a high rate of mobility? If so, this movement may suggest inconsistent educational experiences.), yearly attendance and tardy rates (Is the student frequently absent? Does the student regularly come late to school, perhaps missing literacy instruction on a daily basis?), language survey results (Is the student an English language learner? If so, is he or she receiving language services?), annual classroom grades (Has the student made steady growth, regressed, or flat lined with little change in performance?), formal correspondence between the school and the home (What issues have previous administrators or teachers raised?), and discipline files (Is there a record of the student being disciplined regularly? For major or minor offences?). Current *attendance records* will also disclose the existing consistency with which students come to school . . . and come on time.

All of this information is key to help classroom teachers be cognizant of the story behind the numbers. Students in a classroom may have performed poorly on an assessment, but the task is to look for any extenuating circumstances. Demographic data often change the coaching move made with teachers. Take the example of a classroom of students who received low marks on a state test, but records indicate that the class has a large number of English language learners. Armed with that knowledge, the literacy coach must look beyond the numbers to determine if students under-performed because they lacked the reading skills and competencies expected at that grade or if they lacked language skills. In short, were students proficient in the English language both orally and in academic texts, or were they still trying to navigate a new language? Knowing the answer to those questions dramatically alters coaching moves.

Student Learning Data

Most of the data analysis in schools is directed at student learning, but even here it is imperative that the literacy coach guide teachers not to center their efforts based on a single data point. Student learning data should be conceptualized as a range of interdependent assessments encompassing formative classroom assessments, teacher observations, work samples, summative classroom assessments, and standardized testing.

Formative classroom assessments include quizzes but also encompass the kinds of daily work (e.g., oral questioning, exit cards, self-assessments, hand signals, quick writes) that offer minute-by-minute updates of student learning. This form of data can be particularly beneficial as it is evidence-based and directly informs teaching. *Teacher observations* may not hold the weigh of "hard data," but they offer perceptions of student learning that can often not be obtained any other way. Who better to understand student learning than the teacher who spends every day with them? They also afford the opportunity for teachers to adjust the pacing for the entire class or consider appropriate scaffolding for students who appear to be struggling.

Examining *student work samples* offers another data point to consider. While teacher observation may be more heavily reliant on oral feedback, work samples demonstrate student learning through writing. In addition to what can be ascertained from formative learning assessments, *summative classroom assessments*, like tests and projects, tighten the understanding of what students can do independently.

The final piece is *standardized testing*, whether that be through the school system (often used in universal screenings to determine the academic health of the entire student body) or through state-sponsored high-stakes tests to gauge the academic health of whole school systems.

Collaboration with teachers begins with data. Conversations can contain a variety of questions meant to get to the heart of how classroom teachers can offer prescriptive, targeted support.

- What do standardized test results reveal about student learning?
- Do tests and quizzes align with those results? Yes? What patterns are emerging? No? How are they different? Why might students be performing differently?
- What do work products demonstrate about learning outcomes?
- Are students able to apply skills and competencies independently? If not, why might they be struggling? Where is the disconnect? Where does the skill set break down?
- Are there achievement gaps among particular sub-groups (e.g., ethnicity, gender, income, race)?
- How might instructional practice be adjusted to address areas of concern (or areas of acceleration) identified by the data?

This kind of drilling down can get to what the problem truly is and how the literacy coach can be of assistance in facilitating instructional improvements to meet the specific needs of students.

Behavioral Data

Too often behavioral data are forgotten in the desire to improve student learning outcomes. Academics should never be reviewed in the absence of behavioral records. Behavior has an impetus—be it positive or negative. Students react to a feeling or a situation with a corresponding behavior. It is not uncommon that students misbehave due to their lack of academic skills. Some students become frustrated and act out in class. Others would rather be disciplined than confront the embarrassment of being what they perceive as publicly humiliated for deficits in their literacy skills. It is such a common reality that when principals or teachers remark on misbehaviors, the first data to be considered should be academic performance.

Office referrals can provide information about why students are referred (e.g., inappropriate interactions with students or issues with teachers), when they are referred (e.g., during transitions, in the hallway, during lunch, with particular teachers, or during academic instruction), and how often they are referred (e.g., irregularly, no consistent pattern, or in a recurring time or place). *Classroom discipline* exemplified through time-outs, loss of recess or rewards, calls home, and parent conferences, can also lead to a better understanding of a student.

While behavioral data typically inform on a more individualized basis, some classrooms have entire groups of children misbehaving in such a concerted manner that learning is diminished for all students. In this case, the literacy coach may determine the coaching focus is on teacher actions, student engagement, or appropriate academic rigor before approaching curriculum or instruction. These situations demand a transition from a literacy coach offering content support to an instructional coach who furnishes guidance about classroom management.

There is a great deal to consider when being a data analyst, however this role presents an authentic opportunity to utilize professional tools to create a solution-driven way of approaching instructional improvement. The Student Data Loop is one such instrument and is where formal coaching should begin. Without it, assistance will be offered haphazardly and may or may not be addressing the needs of students. Illustrated in Figure 5.1, the Student Data Loop involves six distinct steps that guide coaching with clarity, intention, and sustained purpose.

1. Step 1 begins with the collection of multiple data sets, looking beyond an individual performance indicator and considering how students are performing on other assessments as well as the underlying factors that may be influencing their learning. This may originate with a high-stakes test or simply a classroom assessment which indicates students are struggling.

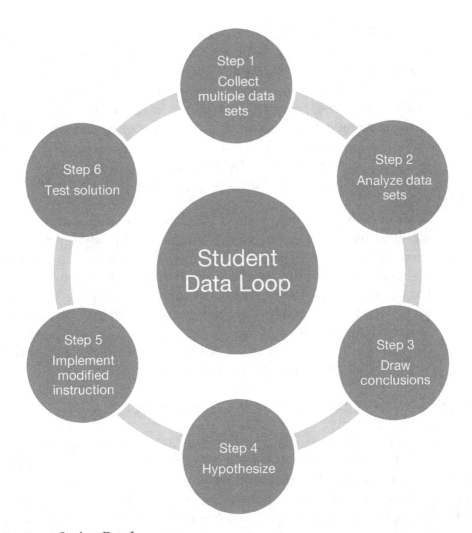

FIGURE 5.1 Student Data Loop

2. In Step 2, the data sets are analyzed—with attention to the purposes for which the information was collected so that the investigation focuses on each data point's insights into student learning as well as inherent limitations.

3. Step 3 requires conclusions to be drawn about what the data suggest, looking beyond the numbers and delving into what those numbers reveal about what students can and cannot do, and, even more importantly, why that may be the case.

4. With a firm grasp of the instructional challenges, Step 4 hypothesizes what potential instructional solution needs to be enacted to respond to the identified need.

5. In Step 5, literacy coaches collaborate with classroom teachers to implement modified instruction to ensure that students are successful—that may require the literacy coach to provide professional learning books, journal articles, or research studies if the teacher lacks the pedagogical foundation to made instructional changes, to model "best practices," to co-plan or co-teach as a scaffolding support, or to build a prescriptive plan incorporating a number of these options. Depending on the complexity of the instructional modification, the coaching cycle may range from 2 to 6 weeks.

6. By Step 6, the classroom teacher assesses students to determine if the hypothesis and recommended instructional modification have been successful. If yes, then the teacher has strengthened his/her instructional repertoire. It not, further collaboration between the literacy coach and classroom teacher needs to take place to determine what may have caused the lack of response to the instructional modification. Was it implemented effectively? Was it indeed the correct hypothesis to make based on the data? Are more data needed to gain a more accurate understanding of student learning?

How Can Literacy Coaches Help Teachers Analyze Data?

Analyzing data is time consuming and requires a skill set beyond the scope of teaching. Because of these demands, many teachers struggle with data analysis and fail to use the information it generates to adjust instructional practices (Herman, Yamashiro, Lefkowitz, & Trusela, 2008; U.S. Department of Education, 2010; Wayman, Cho, & Johnston, 2007). Some teachers also fear that data will be used against them, but "data can make the push for change less personal. The issue isn't about you or me; it's about the goals we're trying to achieve" (Swanson, Allen, & Mancabelli, 2016, p. 68). Keeping student data at the center of conversations with teachers allows the literacy coach to demonstrate the objective purpose of collaboration and the academic benefits students will reap through this partnership.

How are data analyzed? They can be disaggregated by grouping results by performance levels or sub-groups. Another possibility is to consider one set of data within the context of another (e.g., achievement data and attendance statistics, classroom grades and disciplinary referrals). Data should also be actively investigated for patterns and trends. Creating visuals can help in this process as it organizes and reveals insights about student learning outcomes. Visualizing trend lines and charting trajectories also offer the opportunity to view the accumulated effects of current student learning in the future and where gaps manifest and grow.

This all begins, however, with examining student data systematically and routinely. Looking at data should not be a special occasion or be scheduled only after high-stakes tests have been released. It should be a naturally occurring part of ongoing school improvement efforts with student data being regularly analyzed at three distinct levels—at the individual classroom, horizontally among different classrooms in the same grade level, and vertically across multiple grades. At each of these levels, the literacy coach must step outside of the instructional environment and ask "why" we are getting these results.

At the classroom level, the literacy coach works with teachers regularly to analyze how students are performing, considering student-level concerns as well as patterns across the classroom. Analysis shouldn't stop at the final score, but examine how students performed at the item level as well. Are there particular questions or tasks with which students appeared to struggle? Why is that? Were the questions to measure learning aligned to the teaching provided in the classroom? Do students need additional time and modified instructional strategies in order to succeed? The classroom level is where achievement must most closely be scrutinized for it is here where learning takes place and where corrective action will be enacted.

Exploring student learning horizontally among multiple classrooms in a grade yields different, yet highly important, information about grade-level issues. Here is where trends may be discovered, highlighting where the literacy coach and classroom teachers may work together to modify instructional practices for all students. Student need centered within just one classroom can trigger a group discussion about how teachers are offering instruction—what has proven effective and how these practices can be transferred to other classrooms.

Sometimes with assessments characterized by holistic scoring (e.g., essays or projects), the literacy coach can host a "scoring party" with teachers to score student work. Scoring parties can be a simple opportunity to mark student work in a shared setting; however, they have the ability to produce robust study for the teachers in a way that is grounded in student learning. Take the example of an eighth-grade team who met together to look at their students' persuasive essays. Their goal was to calibrate their scoring to ensure a standardized grading system equitable across all of the classrooms. Looking at a single persuasive essay with a scoring rubric of 0 to 6, each teacher reviewed the student's essay and wrote the score on the back. Some variation would be expected, but each teacher assigned a different score. The student's grade ranged from 2 to 6. How is that possible with a shared scoring rubric? The teacher who gave the essay a 6 knew the student personally and explained how far the student had come academically and emphasized that the essay was a huge accomplishment for him. One teacher scored it as a 4 and said that although the rubric criteria would suggest a 3 this was an urban school and it wouldn't be fair to expect the same level for students who faced such disadvantages. A score of 3 was given by a teacher who said that she just scored based on the rubric. The last teacher wrote down a score of 2 because she felt that they should hold their students to high expectations and demand more of them. All of these teachers were passionate about their students. They all believed that their scoring was accurate, but seeing how radically a student's grade may fluctuate based only the difference of a few feet separating classrooms can be an a-ha moment. This one scoring party transformed how these teachers came to understand the process of grading students, the importance of standardizing grading to ensure equity, and the need to look at objective scoring criteria if they were to ensure student growth. Without this horizontal approach to student learning data, these teachers may never have realized how invalid their own data were or learn how to use data effectively as a springboard not only to inform how they grade student work but also to make effective instructional decisions prescriptive to the needs of their students.

Vertical data analysis can reveal equally critical pieces of information—usually systemic areas of need elicited from school-level patterns. Consider the example of an administrator who was encouraging teachers to prepare common assessments about narrative elements across all grade levels and then made a surprising discovery. While their students were making appropriate grade-level benchmarks with that particular skill set, students from all grade levels exhibited an inability to go back to the text and cite evidence to support their responses. This led to a school-wide meeting to determine why students were struggling and then to planning conferences to organize corrective actions at various grade levels. They developed targeted lessons for how to model citing evidence from first grade when students hear read alouds and are asked questions posed by their teachers to intermediate grades when students must compose written responses to secondary students and their ability to quote, paraphrase, or summarize text in defense of their response. By studying student learning data through a team approach, a much more unified, intentional instructional plan evolved that scaffolded student learning across multiple grades.

How Does the Use of Data Drive Coaching?

Data guides decision making in how to support teachers. When thinking about the power of data to influence instructional improvements, the literacy coach should bear in mind that professional development is "less about presenting teachers with a new set of strategies than it is about encouraging them to interrogate and modify strategies" (Whitney et al., 2008, pp. 227–228). How else can classroom teachers interrogate strategies without data to explore, and how would they know what and how to modify these strategies without data as a guide?

Table 5.1 (pages 52–53) highlights some common scenarios, what questions may arise from these situations, and the moves literacy coaches can take to offer prescriptive support for teachers and students. Asking the right questions is how a literacy coach determines an entry point into a classroom. It ensures that effective instructional support is supplied that meets the most pressing needs of students, and by asking these questions and making these coaching moves in concert with teachers the literacy coach forms an inquiry team—a team less concerned about finding fault with teachers and more focused on addressing student learning needs.

These are just some of the more common scenarios literacy coaches come across in the schools in which they work. Whatever situation is encountered, coaching is grounded in data. It functions as the entry point into classroom-embedded professional development, and it will make certain that the work the literacy coach is doing is central to student learning and sustains teacher growth in meaningful ways.

Additional Readings on Data Analysis

Bernhardt, V. L. (2013). *Data analysis for continuous school improvement* (3rd ed.). New York, NY: Taylor & Francis.

Gully, D. D. (2013). Improving instructional practices, policies, and student outcomes for early childhood language and literacy through data-driven decision making. *Early Childhood Education Journal, 41*(6), 413–421.

Holcomb, E. L. (2012). *Data dynamics: Aligning teacher team, school, and district & district efforts.* Bloomington, IN: Solution Tree.

Johnson, R. S., & LaSalle, R. A. (2010). *The wallpaper effect: Data strategies to uncover and eliminate hidden inequities.* Thousand Oaks, CA: Corwin.

Mertler, C. A. (2014). *The data-driven classroom: How do I use student data to drive my instruction?* Alexandria, VA: ASCD Arias.

TABLE 5.1 Data-Driven Coaching Moves

Scenario	Question	Coaching Move
State tests have been released, and a teacher voices concern over her students' performance.	Are students in the class meeting the expected benchmarks?	Examine the results within the context of data sets. How are students performing in other assessment contexts? Identify which students are performing at specific levels (e.g., below basic, basic, proficient, or advanced). Then, determine where students are struggling—with additional assessments if necessary. If multiple concerns arise, begin with the most foundational skills and competencies.
After a high-stakes test, a principal wonders if the school's student achievement levels are comparable to others.	How do students in the class perform in comparison with their grade-level peers in the school? In the school system? Among other schools in the state? In the nation?	Schedule a vertical data analysis meeting. Bring all of the test results including comparison results outside of the school, and search for patterns and trend lines. If discrepancies among grade levels surface, make the entry point in grades and classrooms where instructional strategies can be modified to bring up performance levels comparable to others in the school. If trend lines suggest a school-wide weakness, work collaboratively across the grades to plan how the instructional strategies will differ in various grades and how they should scaffold student instruction.
After reviewing data, a teacher worries that some of her students are not "keeping up" with the others.	How do individual students compare with the class as a whole?	Determine what makes these students different from their peers by studying demographic, student learning, and behavioral data. Pinpoint the variance, and then offer guidance based on the needs of the students. In many cases, students who are struggling will be performing below grade level. If there is to be lasting change for these students, work with the teacher to locate where learning broke down for those students (either through diagnostic assessment or skill assessment).
A principal notes that students have flat lined in her school with students consistently scoring at the same bench-mark level with no appreciable change.	Are students demonstrating improvement over time?	Investigate multiple data sets, but focus on classroom assessments to diagnose student learning needs and establish instructional strategies to respond to those needs.
A teacher sets a goal to improve student comprehension and wonders if what he is doing is really making a difference.	Is instruction improving?	Ensure that the teacher is utilizing best practices and research-based strategies. Analyze classroom assessments to ascertain if student learning is following a positive trajectory. If so, continue with the current instruction. If not, consider alternative strategies that may be more effective.

A teacher complains that he has been focusing on the same instructional objective for weeks, and yet students are not improving.	Why aren't students responding to instruction?	Conference with the teacher about instructional strategies in place. Observe to gain insight into the student experience. Analyze data to establish why students are not responding to instruction. Review assessments item by item to identify patterns and detect points of misunderstanding. Confirm that instruction is appropriate to student need, differentiated for varied learners, engaging, and is aligned with where students are currently functioning. Group students based on common need. Often, teachers attempt to deliver curriculum when students lack the competencies to access content. Support may come in the form of adapting instruction to scaffold students' foundational skills.
A principal asks for support for a teacher who regularly sends students to the office and struggles to maintain control of instruction in the classroom.	Why are students misbehaving?	Analyze all three forms of data: behavioral data, research attendance, and student learning data. Meet with the teacher and observe during literacy instruction. Utilize a "triage" model in which you attack the most problematic that will produce the most change in the quickest amount of time. Begin by pinpointing what is driving student behavior. If it is generated from outside sources, then refer the student to guidance services. If it is based in academic concerns, concentrate on its origin. Teachers who lack classroom management skills will benefit from strategies like organization, procedures and routines, and making transitions run smoothly. Teachers who have students with academic weaknesses that act out due to frustration or humiliation need support in providing differentiated instruction in a caring environment. It may also be a combination of teacher and student needs. In this case, start first with classroom management to gain control of the class as a whole and then move to student learning support.
A teachers asks for help . . . with everything. With such an expansive content area, she simply doesn't know where to begin to offer quality literacy instruction.	Where do you start to design an effective literacy classroom?	Begin with literacy standards. Review what students are expected to learn and work backwards. Examine with the teacher what will have to be in place to ensure that students succeed. Be sure to consider the competency itself (which is the end goal), how the instruction will be delivered (with an organized approach of whole-group, small-group, differentiated, and individualized support), instructional resources that engage and scaffold learning, materials for interventions for struggling students, and ongoing data analysis to track learning.

6

Curriculum Expert
DRIVING QUESTION: What?

As educators, we are only as effective as what we know. If we have no working knowledge of what students studied in previous years, how can we build on their learning? If we have no insight into the curriculum in later grades, how can we prepare learners for future classes?

Heidi Hayes Jacobs

Should a literacy coach be an expert or a learner alongside the classroom teacher? The common view is that literacy coaches should not represent themselves as experts because it damages the relationship they are building with classroom teachers (Toll, 2014). A counter-argument can be made. While no one expects a literacy coach to be an expert in all aspects of literacy, suggesting that coaches are learning about literacy alongside those whom they are purportedly supporting compels others to ask what value they have in the school and in what way they can credibly strengthen teacher learning and growth over that of any other colleague. Classroom teachers come to coaches with the express desire to meet with someone who can enhance their practice in ways that cannot be done on their own. While coaches certainly, themselves, learn from the coaching process—be it new strategies that their classroom partner might employ or insights into teaching and learning not previously recognized—they should not come to the process through the sole stance of a learner. That said, neither is it viable that literacy coaches be knowledgeable about every facet of literacy instruction. It is absolutely appropriate for them to voice when they don't know something. In those situations, they should be honest about their lack of knowledge and affirm that they will get back to the person(s) about a given topic.

COACHING MOVES

- Demonstrate thorough knowledge of current research and pedagogy.
- Dissect standards for better understanding of key knowledge, skills, and learning outcomes.
- Focus coaching on content-specific standards.
- Guide teachers in understanding curriculum.
- Augment teacher content knowledge.
- Support teachers in implementing curriculum.
- Define and make transparent the different curriculum types.
- Assist teachers in delivering the core curriculum.
- Collaborate on assessments that measure student learning of curriculum.

Taking on the role of a curriculum expert, then, answers the question—what?—what level of content knowledge must a literacy coach possess in order to provide effective support for their colleagues? While their understanding cannot be all encompassing, it should definitely equal and exceed that of the classroom teacher whom they are coaching as their role as a curriculum expert centers their credibility and their capacity to support instructional improvement. Focusing on change, building relationships, analyzing data, or for that matter the coaching process itself, has little weight if a coach lacks proficient competence with the curriculum.

What Exactly Is Curriculum and Why Must Literacy Coaches Be Curriculum Experts?

Curriculum can be defined as the learning standards students are expected to meet in a given content and executed through the unit plans and lessons that teachers employ to structure learning, the instructional materials incorporated to strengthen understanding, the assignments through which students demonstrate their grasp of knowledge and skills, and the range of assessments included to measure learning. In essence, curriculum includes every facet of classroom teaching and learning and the professional preparation it requires to ensure student understanding, proficiency, and, eventually, mastery of the content.

Within the content area of literacy instruction, curriculum encompasses the integrated knowledge and skills of reading, writing, speaking, and listening. The professional load is multiplied for coaches by the necessity of being familiar with multiple grade levels, such as in the case of those who serve elementary schools of pre-kindergarten to grade eight students. They must be familiar with a wide swath of curricula—from the emergent literacy of pre-kindergarten and kindergarten up to content area reading of adolescent learners. This can be particularly problematic for coaches whose classroom instruction centered primarily on a particular grade level. For example, coaches who taught exclusively in the primary grades can find it difficult to approach learning standards of middle school students, such as the teaching of argumentative writing. Similarly, coaches who taught at the secondary level often struggle with oral language development and phonics generalizations that typify early childhood education. Because of the expectations placed on literacy coaches to provide support to all teachers, they must familiarize themselves with all grade-level curricula.

This is by no means an easy task, but there are several avenues to build this repertoire, such as subscribing to specialized journals, purchasing professional books, and attending conferences that bridge known deficits in a literacy coach's knowledge base. Talking with a colleague who is a literacy coach with more experience in a particular grade can also be helpful.

Literacy coaches should be aware that curriculum includes a number of key concepts that must be identified and applied if a coach is to develop proficiency and work effectively with teachers from multiple grades. The coach's skill set begins by becoming familiar with the *scope*, or extent, of skills and content that students are expected to learn. Literacy coaches need to be able to identify and explain what students should be learning.

They must also be familiar with the *sequence*, which refers to the vertical order in which different parts of the learning standards are taught. In literacy, sequencing is typically developmental and ordered by pre-requisite skills that students must master in order to progress to the next level in the curriculum.

The horizontal alignment of curriculum is expressed through *integration* of key learning elements with reinforcement and application strategies. Literacy coaches can strengthen integration by working with grade-level teams to map out curriculum and helping them to clarify the learning standards being addressed within their instruction and assessment.

Continuity of vertical alignment of curricular elements necessitates a clear conceptual understanding of how student learning progresses across multiple academic years and how it manifests itself in successive grades as students deepen their understanding of a core concept. For example, the learning standards for narrative elements are profoundly different from the

? COACHING QUESTIONS

(for Teachers)

1. What should students be learning?
2. When should students be learning particular parts of the curriculum?
3. How are learning standards taught?
4. How are students accumulating learning across grade levels?

primary grades to the secondary level. While primary students focus on identifying characters, setting, problem, and solution within a narrative text, older students should no longer require explicit instruction on identification of these narrative elements but rather acquire an understanding of how these elements interact, such as considering how dialogue may divulge aspects of characters not explicitly described by the author. These differences in expectation may appear obvious, but it is not unusual to find middle school students still identifying narrative elements without any deeper prodding as to how they influence story development. It is the literacy coach who must be aware of how curricular objectives change throughout each grade level, helping teachers to offer instruction that is appropriate to the grades they serve—both building on prior learning experiences and preparing students for upcoming expectations.

This begins by obtaining the learning standards for each grade level in which support will be provided and becoming aware of their specific goals, teaching methods, instructional materials, and assessments—meaning the *goals* of the content, the *methods* by which teachers provide instruction, the *materials* which support that learning, and the *assessments* designed to determine student progress. These pieces are not isolated nor are they unrelated to one another. Rather, they function in tandem to build cohesive instruction.

Teachers may need help in identifying appropriate methods or materials for delivering the curriculum, such as how they can assist students in their budding understanding of theme and the texts that may illuminate that understanding for students in their particular grade level. Again, in considering young children, a literacy coach might suggest that the classroom teacher select fables as a strong vehicle to develop a conceptual understanding of theme as this literary genre inherently contains morals that help students begin to understand that stories have lessons and, ultimately, that stories have an underlying meaning beyond just the literal action.

As important as their instructional planning is for delivering curriculum to students, the aspect of assessment cannot be ignored. Teachers benefit from learning how to craft, administer, and interpret assessments as a means to evaluate the effectiveness of their instruction and the progress of student learning. Students must be assessed on the curriculum that is being implemented, and it is the literacy coach who may be needed to offer support as their classroom colleagues strive to construct testing instruments that mirror instruction as well as furnish insights into student learning.

The final issue that coaches must attend to concerns the curriculum delivery system itself and is often a significant issue in schools and class-rooms. Curriculum can be divided into *intended, enacted, assessed,* and *learned curriculum* (Porter & Smithson, 2001). Intended refers to the learning stand-ards and the expectations for what students will learn based on the beliefs of state and local policymakers and described in mandated content standards. Enacted refers to the instruction that actually happens in the classroom—or teachers' practice. Because enacted curriculum is what truly happens in classrooms it is important to be cognizant of its existence as well as how it interplays with the intended curriculum. Being well-informed about the intended curriculum allows coaches to ensure that teachers "enact" instruction that aligns with expectations of the state, school system, and school. The assessed curriculum relates to what is measured—be it state testing or classroom assessments. Learned curriculum, meanwhile, concen-trates on the actual learning students have achieved. In effect, it serves as the product of all of the other types of curriculum delivery. Figure 6.1 illustrates the manner in which these different curriculum types interact and the resulting student learning.

Literacy coaches should be cognizant of these curriculum types as each of them naturally exists in classrooms and the varying degrees of their presence have a profound effect on student learning outcomes. Too often, the intended curriculum put in place by school systems fails to be imple-mented as it was envisioned and, eventually, formally evaluated. In its place, students encounter not the intended curriculum but the enacted curriculum put in place by those who may not have a firm grasp of the grade-level curriculum for which they are responsible to carry out in their classrooms. In that case, the assessed curriculum (at the classroom level) typically links back to the enacted curriculum, which circumnavigates what was originally planned. This scenario is particularly problematic as students encounter standardized assessments and state testing that may not connect

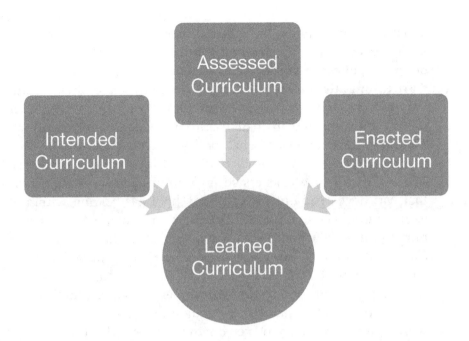

FIGURE 6.1 Curriculum Types

to what they have learned. This disconnect widens the achievement gap in ways that can be avoided if the literacy coach is vigilant in scrutinizing curriculum and managing instructional planning and delivery.

How Can the Role of Curriculum Expert Transform Teaching and Learning?

Leveraging aspects of curriculum has the potential to assert significant influence on school improvement. It requires that literacy coaches move beyond a basic understanding of the curriculum and, instead, shape how instruction is planned, implemented, and assessed through a number of different pathways.

◆ **Curriculum requirements**. The first step is to ensure that classroom teachers have a firm grasp of what the "intended curriculum" entails, which can be realized through a dissection of the standards so that teachers come to a clear understanding of exactly what the standards demand of students at each grade as they progress through the literacy program. What previous learning must they bring with them as prior knowledge in order to build this new learning? What skills and competencies must students learn to master this standard? What skills must they be able to employ independently? What must they be capable of accomplishing in subsequent grades?

◆ **Curriculum alignment**. Building on the knowledge of curriculum requirements and its "intended curriculum" comes how that content will be implemented in their classrooms ("enacted curriculum"). This alignment between what policymakers envision and what teachers practice can be problematic, and it commonly produces a disconnect in which teachers struggle to visualize how curriculum that was developed outside of their school has bearing within the walls of their classrooms. A link between the two emerges from a purposeful, analytical approach to aligning curriculum standards into classroom planning through the use of curriculum mapping. It also allows schools to combine the intended, enacted, and assessed curriculum within one cohesive document. A curriculum map, in essence, plots out "what is being taught over the course of a year, within a unit of study, and even down to a specific lesson" (Johnson, Checkley, & Baker, 2006, p. 2). It may include essential questions, big ideas, a listing of instructional texts, resource materials, assessments, and, hopefully, a plan for how to address students who may struggle with the curriculum or benefit from acceleration. The map is never considered as an end product but as an ongoing preparation for teaching and as an opportunity for consistent collaboration as schools and classrooms evolve. Through the coaching lens, curriculum mapping encourages literacy coaches and classroom teachers (and administrators) to act as a team in deciding what teaching will take place throughout the course of an academic year so that instruction becomes more intentional, planned, and focused. Corresponding to the curriculum map is the pacing guide. Many school systems have enacted these documents to suggest a rate of progress in such a way that all of the teachers who bear responsibility for it devote a consistent amount of time to its delivery. They commonly link to benchmark assessments that allow school systems to monitor student learning. A pacing guide is a practical approach, but it often generates anxiety on the part of classroom teachers who protest that it creates inflexible teaching practices that impede re-teaching or slow curriculum delivery for students who may need more time. A pacing guide also bears the risk of creating a culture of "I've covered it" without the time to ensure that students have actually learned. It is the literacy coach who must help classroom teachers adhere to the standardized expectations of the pacing guide while suggesting resourceful methods for individualization.

◆ **Individualizing curriculum**. While pacing guides can offer a clear "road map" for instructional planning, high-quality curriculum delivery is not realized through a singular approach or expectation. Classroom teachers need to implement ongoing formative assessment to monitor student strengths and target areas for improvement. Potential adjustments to the curriculum include increasing direct instructional time, modifying instructional texts and materials, providing mini-lessons for whole-group instruction that addresses problem spots, strengthening detailed corrective feedback, injecting one-on-one or small-group prescriptive instruc-tion, and analyzing curricular entry points in order to break learning into small, meaningful chunks that are more easily mastered by students.

◆ **Curriculum resources**. The resources to meet curricular needs can have a significant effect on student learning. Literacy coaches must be able to guide classroom teachers in their use of curriculum resources—whether it be textbooks, technology, professional development opportunities, or supplementary materials. These resources must also be aligned—to the curriculum itself and to the needs of students to access the curriculum.

◆ **Curriculum assessment**. While the most common way of assessing curriculum is through high-stakes standardized testing, other less formal assessment techniques to measure student learning should be developed with classroom teachers. It is a valuable task of the literacy coach to characterize assessment not only as a measure-ment of learning outcomes but also as an objective indication of how effectively curriculum is being implemented and how best to adjust instruction to meet the needs of particular classrooms and students.

◆ **Literacy curriculum integration**. Literacy curriculum delivery does not occur in a vacuum. The literacy coach needs to help teachers broaden their vision to include how literacy curriculum can be put into practice within other content areas, such as social studies, science, or math.

In addition, literacy coaches are often invited to help in the selection of core program materials to ensure that they align to curricular objectives, have daily involvement with curriculum as they assist colleagues to group and re-group students, plan instruction, and organize prescriptive intervention support to ensure student mastery of curricular objectives. Taking on the role of a curriculum expert can be awe-inspiring and . . . intimidating. It does not happen overnight, nor does it come easily. Even those experienced in the classroom find the far-reaching demands of curriculum to be daunting. Nevertheless, this is a role that permeates every responsibility that a literacy coach undertakes. Without a knowledge of curriculum, being able to distinguish among its nuances across multiple grades, and speaking knowledgeably about it with colleagues, the effectiveness of the coaching process is significantly impeded.

Additional Readings on Curriculum

Carr, J. F., Herman, N., & Harris, D. E. (2005). *Creating dynamic schools through mentoring, coaching, and collaboration.* Alexandria, VA: ASCD.

Daniels, H., & Zemelman, S. (2014). *Subjects matter: Exceeding standards through powerful content-area reading* (2nd ed.). Portsmouth, NH: Heinemann.

English, F. W. (2010). *Deciding what to teach and test: Developing, aligning, and leading the curriculum* (3rd ed.). Thousand Oaks, CA: Corwin.

Glatthorn, A. A., Boschee, F., Whitehead, B. M., & Boschee, B. F. (2012). *Curriculum leadership: Strategies for development and implementation* (3rd ed.). Thousand Oaks, CA: SAGE Publications, Inc.

Truesdale, V., Thompson, C., & Lucas, M. (2004). *Getting results with curriculum mapping.* Alexandria, VA: ASCD.

7

Resource Manager
DRIVING QUESTION: With What?

In the contemporary teaching and learning environment, every teacher needs to be effective. This demands the tools and resources required to improve practice continuously.

Teaching in the 21st Century

A role embraced by many literacy coaches is that of resource manager. Taking on this responsibility demands coaches be knowledgeable about core programs, supplementary materials, web-based resources, instructional tools, and, pertinent professional information—through books, journals, articles, and research. To excel in this role, however, requires the capability of knowing how to optimize these resources to ensure high-quality instruction.

 COACHING MOVES

◆ Demonstrate knowledge of where to locate appropriate resources for classroom instruction and improving teacher practice.
◆ Seek out resources that will benefit the school, individual classrooms, and the differentiated needs of students.
◆ Locate and provide instructional materials requested by teachers.
◆ Share research and best practices.
◆ Expand the repertoire of instructional resources utilized by teachers.

Classroom teachers frequently visit literacy coaches for the express purpose of locating resources (e.g., manipulatives, an appropriate text for a given lesson, or activity suggestions for a specific learning objective). As beneficial as it is for literacy coaches to be able to identify, locate, and provide appropriate instructional resources for teachers as they plan learning experiences for their students, coaches cannot allow themselves to be placed in this box as their primary role. It is one in which teachers are comfortable and will certainly make their professional lives easier . . . and one in which literacy coaches will feel like everyone's friend and hero. Unfortunately, assuming this role in favor of others allows both the coach and the classroom teacher to escape the tough conversations and hard work necessary to address areas of improvement.

Just how important is this role? It answers the question of "with what" to take up the issue of the instructional resources needed to enhance teachers' practice. Using resources transforms theory about best practice to authentic classroom applications, offers learning opportunities that address the needs of students and not just what is convenient or previously used, broadens teacher thinking about the influence teaching materials have on student engagement and learning outcomes, and modifies instruction in response to data analysis.

How Do Resource Managers Build a School Collection?

Working within this role encompasses a comprehensive array of instructional materials and incorporates elements that may not have been traditionally considered as resources. A literacy coach builds a school's resources and becomes an expert in these resources in three distinct areas: materials that support the curriculum for general instruction; materials that provide tools to remediate the curriculum for students who are struggling; and materials that present the opportunity to enrich the curriculum to create accelerated learning experiences (see Figure 7.1).

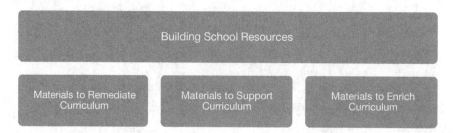

FIGURE 7.1 Building School Resources

Assembling the appropriate resources for a school can be somewhat generic in the sense that high-caliber resources share similar characteristics for all schools; however, other resources will need to be amassed based on analyzing student assessments and providing tools to address those particular needs and support instructional improvement.

What Kinds of Resources Are Important?

Some resources can be easily collected or even already within the possession of the literacy coach; while others demand pre-planning and intentional organization for the specific needs of a school. There are, however, certain resources that all literacy coaches should have on hand to meet the daily needs of their colleagues.

- **Professional conferences**. Professional conferences (locally, regionally, nationally, and internationally) and upcoming professional meetings posted for teachers' attention often spur teachers to seek more formalized growth opportunities. Colleagues may also inquire about professional development that would help them improve their skills in particular topics, such as differentiation, guided reading, or writing. Within the field of reading and writing, the International Literacy Association (ILA) hosts annual conferences in the United States and around the world in addition to their state-led conferences and local council offerings. Regional educational centers also provide sessions—some as brief as only a few hours.
- **Professional books**. Most literacy coaches have built their own professional library well before assuming an instructional leadership

? COACHING QUESTIONS

1. What resources currently exist in the school? (for Administrators, Teachers, and Literacy Coaches)
2. What potential resources are needed to fill a gap to enhance teaching and learning? (for Administrators, Teachers, and Literacy Coaches)
3. How will resources be made available to classroom teachers? (for Administrators and Literacy Coaches)
4. In what ways may resources be used in the coaching process? (for Literacy Coaches)

role within a school. They often continue to add to their collection as they encounter issues that may not have arisen in their own professional experience. If planning for a balanced assortment of books, topics should include early childhood learning needs, vocabulary, comprehension, fluency, struggling readings, writing instruction, the literacy block, differentiation, reading across the curriculum, raising rigor, English-language learners, and any other topics that address the unique needs of the schools they serve.

◆ **Professional journals**. Being aware of current issues in teaching and learning as well as in literacy is a non-negotiable responsibility of the literacy coach. One key method to achieve this is through subscriptions to professional journals. Reading journals will not only ensure that the coach is current but also provide additional resources for colleagues—whether it be through a lending library in which teachers can "check out" professional journals as a means to keep their skill set current or through selecting journal articles that speak to issues as they surface. Subscriptions to *Educational Leadership, The Reading Teacher*, the *Journal of Adolescent and Adult Literacy, Reading Research Quarterly*, and the *Journal of Literacy Research* are high-quality publications from which to start. Another interesting option is the Marshall Memo distributed by Kim Marshall who subscribes to over 60 publications and then summarizes 5–10 articles each week that he believes have the power to improve teaching and learning. His weekly memo arrives in the subscriber's email along with article e-links and access to the over 6,000 article summaries he has written since its inception in 2003.

◆ **Research articles**. A primary task of literacy coaches is to build not only relational trust but also professional trust. It is not enough to share personal experiences and opinions; coaches must ground their collaboration in what current research validates. In this endeavor, coaches should be cognizant of key issues addressed in the school and compile professional writing that authenticates instructional changes. Possible journals to build a collection of current research writings come from the *Journal of Literacy Research*, the *Journal of Research in Reading, Literacy Research and Instruction, Reading Research Quarterly*, and *Reading and Writing*.

◆ **On-line articles**. For those who may find professional journal subscriptions too costly, on-line articles offer a simple alternative. They also present the added benefit of being highly current. Care should be taken, although, to choose articles with the domain suffix of .gov (government entity) or .edu (educational institution), which ensure a more balanced approach rather than a domain suffix of .com, which should be reviewed more carefully as it represents a commercial, for-profit organization or of .org representing a non-profit group—both of which may have a particular bias or represent a particular point of view. *Education Week* has a subscription for national and state news related to the field of education so that literacy coaches can be aware of significant new legislation, current trends, and educational reports being released. In addition to the physical newspaper, *Education Week* also has a service for a free daily e-newsletter, blogs, and videos.

◆ **Internet links**. Web- and technology-based solutions offer up-to-the-moment, easily accessible supports that can facilitate planning and instruction. These links may focus on more professional writings or provide student materials. Teachers in search of instructional support through lesson planning ideas may benefit from ReadWriteThink.org. For student needs, Reading A-Z, if purchased, offers thousands of leveled readers in English and Spanish, lesson plans, and assessments—beginning with phonemic awareness activities and extending to upper elementary content area and genre collection studies. Likewise, Newsela.com (at no charge) provides leveled news articles and text sets, in English and Spanish, that allow the user to keep the core content while adjusting the readability among varied text complexity levels so that teachers can differentiate their texts to the needs of their students. Smithsonian Tween Tribune (at no cost) offers multiple texts of varied readability levels as well but also includes a limited selection of lesson plans.

◆ **Children's books**. Books for students are always in demand in the classroom. Teachers often come in search of books for guided reading, literature circles, book clubs, independent reading, mentor texts, or other text-based activities. Children's books can be organized by readability, fiction versus information, genre, themes, or other pertinent characteristics unique to the school's needs. The purchase of books should be made in conjunction with the teachers who will utilize them to ensure collaboration among adults and usefulness for children.

◆ **Book rooms**. On a grander scale, a book room offers a shared reading resource for the entire school. Housed in a common site available for everyone's use, it functions as a lending library so that teachers have access to a broad range of high-quality books, ensuring their ability to provide differentiated, prescriptive reading experiences for students. Creating a book room encourages collaboration, allows teachers to pool their resources, and provides a meeting place to discuss books and learning. Care should be taken to ensure that the books represent a balance—fiction and nonfiction, text sets, books that have phonics features, guided reading books, shared reading books, mentor texts, independent reading books, and books that are culturally responsive—as well as professional resources. It is the literacy coach who has the influence to propose the benefits of a book room, use school funds to stock it with appropriate materials, help to organize it to establish its functionality, and guide their colleagues in making the most of its contents.

◆ **Manipulatives**. Students benefit from manipulative-based reading instruction as they link the abstract to the concrete through active, engaging experiences. A basic list of materials includes phoneme picture cards, letter tiles, magnetic letters, Play-Doh for letter formation, word building kits, sight word materials, magnetic prefixes, suffixes, and root words, games, and white boards and markers for small-group instruction.

◆ **Assessments**. An ongoing complaint about today's educational culture is that high-stakes testing has narrowed the curriculum and obliged too much time devoted to test preparation. Informal, classroom-based assessments, however, are an essential aspect of expert instruction. The learning profile gleaned from these tools allows teachers to quantify learning, to diagnose student strengths and weaknesses, and to prepare prescriptive instructional experiences unique to individual student needs. Classroom teachers often ask their literacy coaches for help in assessing their students in phonological awareness, vocabulary, and comprehension. For literacy coaches who do not already have a range of assessments, they can easily be obtained on the Internet from free websites.

The role of resource manager is an important one. It can open doors to teachers who may otherwise be reluctant to work with literacy coaches but welcome the innocuous support of having additional resources at their disposal. It also serves as a means to support instructional improvement and learning opportunities based on student need. Essentially, being a resource manager allows the literacy coach to collaborate with his or her classroom colleagues about important issues in teaching and learning—like strong core instructional practices, flexible grouping for student learning, differentiation strategies, and the importance of ongoing professional growth. So, resource managers are popular, but they also can bring about genuine change in a school's learning culture.

Additional Readings on Resources

Galda, L., Liang, L. A., & Cullinan, B. E. (2017). *Literature and the child* (9th ed.). Boston, MA: Cengage Learning.

Graham, S., MacArthur, C. A., & Fitzgerald, J. (Eds.). (2013). *Best practices in writing instruction* (2nd ed.). New York, NY: Guilford Press.

Taylor, B. M., & Duke, N. K. (Eds.). (2013). *Handbook of effective literacy instruction: Research-based practice k-8*. New York, NY: Guilford Press.

Walentas, N. (2009). *Reading manipulatives sourcebook: Practical strategies, materials and resources for teaching all levels of literacy skills*. Phoenix, AZ: Reading Manipulatives.

William, D., & Leahy, S. (2015). *Embedding formative assessment: Practice techniques for k-12 classrooms*. West Palm Beach, FL: Learning Sciences International.

8

Instructional Specialist
DRIVING QUESTION: How?

Simply put, those who assume literacy leadership must be experts in the field of literacy.

Jill Lewis-Spector and Annemarie B. Jay

At the central point of coaching is student learning which is why one of the primary roles that literacy coaches maintain is that of instructional specialist. Keeping this role central to the coaching process creates a positive correlation between coaches and student achievement (Blachowicz, Obrochta, & Fogelberg, 2005). The driving question for being an instructional specialist is—how? How do literacy coaches create and sustain meaningful change in teaching and learning within a school?

 COACHING MOVES

- Demonstrate comprehensive knowledge of evidence-based practices.
- Use assessment to drive coaching and instruction.
- Observe and provide feedback based on measurable objectives.
- Collaborate in planning and delivery of lessons (short-term objectives) and units (long-range goals).
- Model well-designed lessons.
- Aid teachers in forming instructional groups.
- Suggest appropriate differentiated practices.
- Stay abreast of technology.
- Pose questions that elicit reflection and is solution-driven.
- Focus on using assessment for learning.

The answer begins with how classroom teachers perceive their literacy coach. If classroom teachers believe that their coach has a strong knowledge base about literacy education and skilled expertise to help them, they typically rate them as more capable to influence instructional change and subsequently have a more significant impact on teacher practice (L'Allier, Elish-Piper, & Bean, 2010; Marsh et al., 2012). This credibility, in turn, allows the literacy coach to be more successful in bringing evidence-based practices into classrooms to enhance teacher capacity and increase student achievement.

How Important Is the Role of Instructional Specialist?

Instruction consumes a great deal of time and work within the schedule of a literacy coach. All of the other roles—change agent, relationship builder, data analyst, curriculum expert, resource manager, and professional developer—serve to consolidate the capability of literacy coaches to act as instructional specialists and make real, sustainable improvements to teacher practice. This focus on instruction is where the effects of coaching can be made visible through changes in both teaching and learning, as evidenced by student achievement. Without changes in how students are performing, there is little reason for the presence of literacy coaches. It is, in truth, their primary purpose for existing in schools and classrooms.

What Does an Instructional Specialist Do?

Instructional specialists are knowledgeable about the pedagogy of literacy instruction and have a repertoire of "best practice" strategies to address the diverse needs of students across a range of grade levels and learning environments. Equally important, they have the ability to share this knowledge with their colleagues in ways that make sense and are easily transferrable to others' instructional approaches. Instructional specialists, then, must have two key talents—possessing their own expert understanding of instruction and being able to impart that knowledge skillfully to their classroom colleagues.

They sharpen their usefulness in this role by *maintaining a consistent focus on improving pedagogical practice.* The varied roles and responsibilities that literacy coaches sustain can often divert attention from the real work to be done in schools and classrooms, but their role as an instructional specialist centers efforts on teaching and learning. While "teaching and learning" has become a ubiquitous—and sometimes empty—educational term, these two

❓ COACHING QUESTIONS

(for Literacy Coaches)

1. What is the objective of my work with classroom teachers?
2. How do I establish a culture of instructional improvement?
3. How important is student data to my work with classroom teachers?
4. What process guides implementation of strategy development in classrooms?

processes feed off of one another. They cannot exist without the other, and they can neither fail nor succeed without the other's presence. If it is understood that the primary purpose of a literacy coach is to raise student achievement, then that task is not possible without addressing the other half of the equation—teachers.

The broad goal of coaching centers on an aspect of instruction that supports student growth, but the specific objective of that endeavor is the instructional strategy or technique that is collaboratively determined to be learned or improved upon as a result of that work. Take the scenario of a second-grade teacher who comes to his literacy coach because of low oral reading fluency scores. He is distraught about his students' performance and watches them struggle during guided reading; however, he is uncertain about the reasons for their dysfluency as well as possible techniques to address it. He and his literacy coach first talk about the three components of fluent reading (i.e., accuracy, automaticity, and prosody) and then sit together to complete running records of students reading. Later in the day, they meet again to analyze the student results and note that students are lacking prosody (expressive reading) but identify a more serious causal factor affecting fluency. Students can accurately identify words but they lack automaticity, instead reading slowly word by word. Upon a thorough examination of the running records, they determine the primary deficit that his students have is word recognition created by their lack of a solid mastery of phonics generalizations. Students are sounding out each word with painstaking effort. They decide to focus on embedding phonics patterns in daily instruction with meaningful texts. The literacy coach helps him to plan his literacy block to include whole-group instruction on phonics, to reinforce it in his guided reading groups with naturally occurring examples, and to provide independent practice with phonic readers and hands-on activities—all building to automaticity so that students decode words with less effort. To demonstrate how these elements can be implemented without fragmenting the work that he is already doing, the literacy coach co-plans a lesson, co-teaches with him, and then continues to provide feedback as she visits the room. They continue to collaborate, meeting regularly to monitor student progress, and, consequently, the effectiveness of the instructional strategies being put in place in his classroom. In this scenario, the goal was oral reading fluency, but the coaching objective for their work together was to implement prescriptive strategies within the literacy block to enhance students' automaticity when reading.

In order for this caliber of work to flourish, the literacy coach must *establish a school culture of ongoing instructional improvement*. Decisions about student achievement should be grounded in the belief that instruction has the power to make a difference in how students learn and how they perform academically. If that conviction is held by school members, then a natural byproduct of that principle is that to change student outcomes teaching must first be changed. Thus, literacy coaches consistently examine student data with their classroom colleagues to pinpoint student deficits and then collaborate on instructional practices to address these gaps.

A culture of continuing learning and growth comes about when the literacy coach *stays informed on national and state standards as well as current issues and best practices in instructional methods*. It is essential that the literacy coach has a firm grasp on standards and is accustomed to how they evolve from grade to grade. Helping classroom teachers understand how the standards should manifest themselves in their classrooms as well as how their students will be assessed on those standards is pivotal to skillful, grade-appropriate instruction. Teachers are often familiar with the anchor standards that link across multiple grades but don't recognize the nuances within grade levels. For example, while an anchor standard for all grades might encompass the broad umbrella of text structure, one grade might focus on how chapters, scenes, and stanzas provide structure to stories, dramas, and poems. Another grade might emphasize how those pieces contribute to the development of theme, and yet another may require students to analyze two different texts to determine how the different structures inherent in the two texts influence meaning or style. Understanding how distinctive targeted learning outcomes may be across grade levels and then distinguishing the unique instructional practices to support that learning ensures that classroom teachers are providing skillful learning experiences.

In addition to national and state standards, the literacy coach must base the work of coaching on a clear link to the school's program and awareness of teacher competence in delivering that program to students. Each school is unique in both its constitution and its approach to teaching and learning. A literacy coach must be aware of the program focus of the school and, equally importantly, the competencies of classroom colleagues. Just as teachers scaffold their students in a classroom, a coach must be cognizant of the professional capacity of teachers and be prepared to meet each of them wherever they may currently be operating. Some teachers may benefit from more sophisticated practices, while others need foundational instructional principles to support their work.

Think back to the scenario about the teacher who sought assistance with fluency. This is not an uncommon focus area for primary teachers, and it may easily be a concern for other teachers in his grade. What is important to understand as a literacy coach, however, is that instructional strategies differ widely among teachers. A novice teacher may be uncertain how to address fluency and be searching for a simple strategy to implement that won't be too challenging in the face of a tough first year of teaching. The coach, in this instance, might suggest one strategy, like repeated readings or Readers' Theater. Another more seasoned teacher might have used these strategies frequently in the past and be looking for something more sophisticated. To respond to this very different need, the literacy coach might suggest Fluency-Oriented Reading Instruction (FORI) as described by Stahl and Heubach in 2005, which constitutes multiple days of re-reading both in school and at home, creating a unit approach to fluency instruction. Thus, the teachers have the same instructional need, but the tactic taken by the literacy coach addresses their professional capacity and fits their unique teaching skill set.

Analyzing district and school data as well as current research theory and application should also be an element under consideration when attempting to improve instructional sequence, content delivery, and the results of the teaching and learning taking place in classrooms. Being cognizant of how students are performing paired with evidence-based practices allow the literacy coach to help classroom teachers link curriculum to the learning needs of students. This relates directly to the role of data analyst, using the insights garnered from student performance to help teachers address learning deficits prescriptively and efficiently.

On a day-to-day basis, the work of coaching centers on *collaborating with teachers to design, implement, and evaluate instructional units and lessons.* This work includes examining learning objectives to ensure that they are pertinent to the grade level, related to the greater unit goals, specific (e.g., students will be able to determine importance in a selected passage versus students will improve their reading comprehension), and measurable (e.g., students will be able to identify unfamiliar words using context clues versus students will use vocabulary to understand the text). The literacy coach also works with teachers to identify and refine the implementation of instructional strategies and to select instructional materials that will help students achieve learning objectives. Importantly, attention must also be paid to the assessments (e.g., formative and summative) that will be used to determine if the instructional strategies have been successful.

As classroom teachers build their instructional capacity, the literacy coach also *analyzes instruction for cognitive engagement and cognitive demand.* Just how important is cognitive engagement? A Gallup survey (Lopez & Calderon, 2011) revealed that an average of 45 percent of students labeled themselves as not engaged or actively disengaged from learning. With nearly half of students voicing a disconnect to their own academic experiences, how teachers approach planning and delivery of content is crucial. Unit planning and lesson planning should encompass not just the content to be learned but also how engaged students are in tasks and learning experiences and the degree of cognitive demand present in questioning, tasks, and assessments.

Collaborative work should revolve around three key dimensions of engagement: behavioral engagement (e.g., how students behave in the classroom and lack of disruptions); emotional engagement (e.g., the level of comfort or interest a student exhibits); and, finally, cognitive engagement (e.g., student capacity to reflect, adapt, and deepen their learning). These seemingly distinct facets of engagement bind together to strengthen student learning and academic success (Fredricks, Blumenfeld, & Paris 2004). The literacy coach helps classroom teachers gauge how intently students are connecting with the lesson through instructional practices like student choice, project-based learning, culturally-appropriate instruction, cognitively challenging tasks, technology to strengthen learning experiences and exploration, and the creation of a safe environment in which students are encouraged to explore and make mistakes as an accepted practice in the acquisition of learning (NASBE, 2015).

What's more, research over the past quarter of a century has consistently suggested that students learn best in classrooms that integrate cognitively demanding instruction throughout lesson delivery (Kessler, Stein, & Schunn, 2015). Using a metric is one way to maintain attention on ensuring cognitive demand. The literacy coach and classroom teacher may elect to use Bloom's Taxonomy or Webb's Depth of Knowledge levels, but cognitive demand in classrooms naturally increases when students transition from rote recall of content to application of learning and explanation of their own thinking.

As classroom sizes continue to grow, teachers must also address the variance of learners for whom they are academically responsible. They must scaffold students who are functioning below their grade level to strengthen their abilities and move them closer to grade-appropriate performance; they need to provide high-quality instruction for those students on grade level to ensure that they continue to learn and grow intellectually, and they must not lose sight of academically gifted students who need enrichment in order to thrive. This is a daunting task and is what typically distinguishes a good teacher from a great teacher. The means by which a literacy coach can help a good teacher become a great teacher is through *differentiating instructional practices*.

This in itself can be a difficult process and not one easily mastered. It begins, however, with an understanding of the elements of classroom differentiation, which Carol Ann Tomlinson has eloquently described over the course of the last decades—through content (what the student will learn or how they will gain access to learning experiences), process (learning activities for students to help them make sense of the content), product (culminating assessments that allow students to show what they have learned), and environment (establishing how the classroom looks and operates) (Tomlinson, 2000). Providing such a structure brings order and clarity to tailoring instruction for student needs.

Literacy coaches can use Tomlinson's work to help classroom teachers determine which element might be adjusted in the classroom that would best serve the needs of their students. For content modification, that might mean that teachers use differentiated vocabulary lists based on the readiness levels of their students rather than expecting all students to be equally challenged by the same word lists. It may also take place through texts at varied readability levels so that all students can access learning materials. In the area of process, teachers may provide explicit instruction, modeling, or manipulatives for those students who may benefit from concrete representations of literacy concepts. Products can be differentiated by allowing students to have multiple avenues to demonstrate their learning (e.g., traditional paper and pencil tests, oral presentations, or artistic representations like poster projects or murals). The learning environment can be modified to allow for quiet spaces for individual work or areas conducive for collaboration. Whatever element is selected for differentiation, the literacy coach should focus on how that particular element of instructional practice aligns to the needs of students.

Another avenue to instructional improvement is through *looking at student work protocols*. Examining work samples provides comprehensive insight into both teaching and learning. It furnishes a structure by which literacy coaches and their classroom colleagues can scrutinize student work to gain a better understanding of what students are thinking and how they understand content. By holding collaborative sessions, it also encourages a collective approach so that multiple teachers can analyze and give their own unique perspective as to what the work samples reflect as well as what instructional modifications they would recommend to support student learning where it currently exists. What's more, its outcome supports the work of the individual teacher as that teacher now has increased the expertise from which change can be drawn. See Chapter 9 for recommended Looking at Student Work (LASW) protocols and suggestions for embedding this tool in professional development opportunities.

How Does an Instructional Specialist Employ Strategies Prescriptively?

There are countless strategies being carried out in schools and classrooms on any given day of the school year—some are commonly used and identified as best practice while others are less known or perhaps based on recent research, of which only those who keep abreast of the most up to-date studies may be aware. With so many possibilities, how does a literacy coach make cogent decisions when supporting instructional improvement?

It begins with *maintaining a consistent focus on improving pedagogical practice and establishing a school culture of ongoing instructional improvement* so that the professional environment is receptive to learning and growth. To accomplish this goal, the literacy coach must *stay informed on national and state standards as well as current issues and best practices in instructional methods* and *base the work of coaching on a clear link to the school's program and awareness of teacher competency in delivering that program to students*. With these elements in place, an effective literacy coach *analyzes district and school data as well as current research theory and application* to help teachers adjust instruction to meet the needs of their students. It is here that true decision making begins. To provide prescriptive, differentiated support for individual teachers, the literacy coach utilizes this data analysis to determine—in partnership with the classroom teacher—what the objective of their work will be and what outcome they are seeking as a result of that work. Based on that decision, the literacy coach can identify one of the following options to utilize in this collaborative endeavor:

◆ Collaborating with teachers to design, implement, and evaluate instructional units and lessons.
◆ Analyzing instruction for cognitive engagement and cognitive demand.
◆ Differentiating instructional practices.
◆ Looking at student work.

Using data analysis and these focal points as a guide allows the literacy coach to pinpoint exact targets for instructional improvement in an organized, coherent approach that centers on the individual teacher competencies and student learning.

Additional Readings on Instructional Improvement

Blythe, T., Allen, D., & Schieffelin Powell, B. (2015). *Looking at student work* (3rd ed.). New York, NY: Teachers College Press.

Ferlazzo, L. (2013). *Classroom management Q & As: Expert strategies for teaching.* Bethesda, MD: Educational Week Press.

Grant, L. W., Hindman, J. L., & Stronge, J. H. (2013). *Planning, instruction, and assessment: Effective teaching practices.* New York, NY: Routledge. (Original work published 2010)

Marzano, R. J., & Pickering, D. J. (2011). *The highly engaged classroom.* Bloomington, IN: Marzano Research Laboratory.

Tomlinson, C. A. (2014). *The differentiated classroom: Responding to the needs of all learners* (2nd ed.). Alexandria, VA: ASCD.

Walsh, J. A., & Sattes, B. D. (2011). *Thinking through quality questioning: Deepening student engagement.* Thousand Oaks, CA: Corwin.

9

Professional Developer

DRIVING QUESTION: How Well?

We will . . . fail to improve schooling for children until we acknowledge the importance
of schools not only as places for teachers to work but also for teachers to learn.
Mark Smylie

The role of professional developer is the most commonly recognized
responsibility of a literacy coach. It can also, however, be one of the most
challenging aspects of the position. In this circumstance, the question
transitions from "how" to "how well" change can be realized. It compels a
literacy coach not just to be a curriculum expert or an instructional specialist;
it demands the ability to impart this professional knowledge in a way that
is conducive to adult learning and in varied contexts so that classroom
teachers have multiple pathways by which to grasp new learning, embed it
in their practice, and be willing to embrace what may be unfamiliar and
constitute risk-taking on their part. To be an effective professional developer,
one must first understand why adult learning is so important to student
learning, how adult learning experiences differ from student learning
experiences, what potential forms professional development might take and
recognize when one is more powerful and more appropriate than another,
and what features ensure a highly effective professional development
program . . . one designed and implemented to engender transformative
change in schools and in classrooms.

COACHING MOVES

- ◆ Understand how adults learn.
- ◆ Administer professional development needs survey.
- ◆ Nurture a culture of professional inquiry.
- ◆ Develop a professional development plan based on evidence-based needs of students and teachers.
- ◆ Offer a range of professional development opportunities (e.g., faculty workshop, teacher study group, lesson study, coaching cycles suited to student learning needs, coaching goals, and individual teacher practice).
- ◆ Engage in coaching rotations that include coaching cycles (for all teachers) as well as consultancies (both teacher-driven and administrative referrals).

How Significant Is Professional Development?

Research has consistently found that teacher quality acts as a lever for student learning and is often considered as the single greatest factor influencing student achievement (Alliance for Excellent Education, 2006; Boston Public Schools, 1998; Darling-Hammond, 1999; Goe & Stickler, 2008; Hightower et al., 2011; Jordan et al., 1997; Rowan, Correnti, & Miller, 2002; Sanders & Rivers, 1996; Wright, Horn, & Sanders, 1997; Yoon et al., 2007) and that with intensive mentoring novice teachers can begin to produce significant results with student learning within 2 years (Strong, Fletcher, & Villar, 2004). Just how important is teacher quality? From a landmark study in 1997, researchers Wright, Horn, and Sanders noted the following:

> the results of this study well document that the most important factor affecting student learning is the teacher. In addition, the results show wide variation in effectiveness among teachers. The immediate and clear implication of this finding is that seemingly more can be done to improve education by improving the effectiveness of teachers than by any other single factor. Effective teachers appear to be effective with students of all achievement levels, regardless of the level of heterogeneity in their classrooms.

(p. 63)

This conviction was echoed in 1998 by a well-known study conducted by Richard F. Elmore and Deanna Burney, which asserted that "there is growing consensus among educational reformers that professional development for teachers and administrators lies at the center of the educational reform and instructional improvement" (p. 1).

School systems generally employ professional development as a universal strategy to improve teacher quality, encouraging ongoing inquiry into teaching practices and consistent improvement in student learning. Looking at it through a coaching lens, it allows a literacy coach to facilitate instructional reform by connecting classroom teachers in continual professional learning that is school-specific and often teacher-specific—not something attainable by a university course, a conference, or professional book (Bean et al., 2010; Gibson, 2006). The literacy coach is in a unique position to offer individualized, targeted learning opportunities and, thus, has the greatest likelihood to produce change that is relevant and sustainable.

How does it work? Yoon and colleagues (2007) examined 1,300 studies about the influence of professional development and determined that with intensive professional development—on average approximately 49 hours—teachers can raise student achievement by 21 points on standardized testing. The researchers found that professional development incorporating less than 14 hours was ineffective and produced no change in student learning. The common denominator in all of these scenarios is the literacy coach who is in a position to provide school-based, intensive professional learning opportunities (Dole, 2004; Hawley & Valli, 1999; Sykes, 1999).

Mizell (2010) sums it up this simply: "Educators who do not experience effective professional development do not improve their skills, and student

? COACHING QUESTIONS

1. Is there an intentional plan for professional development? (for Administrators and Literacy Coaches)
2. Does professional learning align with the change efforts in place to support the school's vision? (for Administrators and Literacy Coaches)
3. How does professional learning link to research on adult learning? (for Literacy Coaches)
4. Is the professional development plan producing changes in student learning? (for Administrators and Literacy Coaches)

learning suffers" (p. 6). Joyce and Showers (2002), the originators of peer coaching, make their case even more strongly—"student achievement is the product of formal study by educators" (p. 3). So it is imperative that literacy coaches never lose focus that while their goal is to increase student achievement, that target can never be reached without first recognizing the importance of teacher learning.

In What Ways Do Adults Learn and How Does This Influence Professional Development?

There are several learning theories that relate directly to adults. The work of Knowles furnishes general principles associated with adult learners; Kolb suggests how adults transition through new learning; and Honey and Mumford offer learning style preferences. Using these theories in tandem provides a framework for planning professional development that is appropriate for teachers at all stages of their professional careers (Trotter, 2006).

Perhaps the most recognized approach to adult learning comes from Malcolm Knowles. The term andragogy, the study of adult learning, was first authored in 1833 in Germany and was later introduced in the United States by Edward Lindeman in 1926, but it was Malcolm Knowles, an American educator, who pioneered the *Theory of Andragogy* and characterized it as the "art and science of helping adults learn" (Knowles, 1980, p. 43). The concept of andragogy (the theories and methods of teaching adult learners) contrasts with pedagogy (the theories and methods of teaching children) and makes distinctions about assumptions for older learners.

He posited that adult learners have specific characteristics, including the precepts that adult learners are self-directed, use their own knowledge base, are goal- and relevancy-oriented, focus on practicality, and prefer collaboration. Knowles also suggested that there are four principles applied to adult learning. First, adults need to be involved in planning their learning experiences. This aligns to the importance of classroom teachers being involved in setting the vision of a school and viewing themselves as active participants in the change process as well as their own professional learning. Second, experience forms the foundation of learning—including the mistakes made when implementing something new. This experiential approach to professional learning accounts for the benefits of classroom-embedded coaching in which they collaborate with their literacy coach to apply new strategies and techniques into their practice. Third, adults are most interested in learning that has an immediate, direct link to their work. Developing a professional development plan based on the school's vision and linked to student achievement allows teachers to visualize how their own learning opportunities will assist them in their classrooms. Fourth, learning is problem-centered rather than content-centered. Thus, while professional development may pivot on literacy, teacher engagement increases as teachers come to view learning as a means to solve problems in student learning (Knowles, 1984a, 1984b). This need for self-direction and autonomy has significant implications on the work that literacy coaches engage in with teachers as Knowles and his colleagues (1998) explain.

> Once they (adults) have arrived at the (independent) self-concept they develop a deep psychological need to be seen by others and treated by others as being capable of self-direction. They resent and resist situations in which they feel others are imposing their wills on them. This presents a serious problem in adult education: the minute adults walk into an activity labeled "education," "training," or anything synonymous, they hark back to their conditioning in their previous school experience.
>
> (p. 65)

Andragogy, then, underscores the distinction between student learners and adult learners (Taylor & Kroth, 2009) as well as the necessity for collaboration and joint endeavors rather than administrators and leadership teams making decisions without input and participation about classroom teachers.

This sense of autonomy and the need for relevant experiences are further emphasized by Kolb's *Experiential Learning Theory* (1984) in which he argues that adults learn as they transition among four different cycles, which are continuous and can be entered at any stage; however, learners must engage in all four for effective learning to take place. The four stages are Concrete Experience (i.e., learning from experiences and relations with others), Reflective Observation (i.e., observing through multiple perspectives), Abstract Conceptualization (i.e., understanding the theory behind new learning), and Active Experimentation (i.e., implementing new learning). These stages can be scaffolded through the range of professional development experiences that a literacy coach can offer. Table 9.1 demonstrates how these experiences might align to Kolb's theory.

While any of the learning experiences listed in Table 9.1 can be modified to address the four stages of learning, they inherently lend themselves to particular stages based on their focus. For example, attending a faculty

TABLE 9.1 Kolb's Experiential Learning Style Theory Aligned to Professional Development

	Abstract Conceptualization "Thinking" (Learn from listening to others and from professional readings)	Reflective Observation "Watching" (Observe others, think about own practice, and make meaning)	Concrete Experience "Feeling" (Receive practical recommendations; engage in new practice with support)	Active Experimentation "Doing" (Try out new teaching practice with independence)
Faculty Workshop	X			
Team Meeting	X			
Classroom Visitation	X	X		
Teacher Study Group	X	X	X	
Observation & Feedback Loop	X	X	X	
Modeling	X	X		
Co-Planning	X	X		
Co-Teaching	X	X	X	
Lesson Study	X	X	X	X
Looking at Student Work	X	X	X	
Examining Achievement Data	X	X	X	
Coaching Cycle				X
Pre-Conference	X			
Observation		X		
Post-Conference			X	

workshop may provide abstract conceptualization, but it is less likely to offer participants opportunities to reflect or try out their new learning. In contrast, lesson study and the coaching cycle offer transition through all four stages. In some instances, only one form of professional development is necessary. It should be noted, however, that a professional development plan for long-term school-wide goals should permeate the school learning culture and might link several different forms of professional development and utilize them in unique contexts to offer participants multiple pathways to achieve the goal of sustained instructional improvement, such as in the examples below.

◆ **Learn how to differentiate vocabulary instruction.**
  ◆ *Abstract Conceptualization*: Faculty Meeting to describe rationale and process.
  ◆ *Reflective Observation*: Classroom Visitation to see it implemented by others.
  ◆ *Active Experimentation*: Coaching Cycle to get feedback on implementation.
  ◆ *Concrete Experience*: Look at Student Work for possible modifications.

◆ **Learn to administer running records.**
  ◆ *Reflective Observation*: Model the assessment administration.
  ◆ *Abstract Conceptualization*: Team Meeting to discuss assessment administration.
  ◆ *Concrete Experience*: Co-Teach (co-administer) assessment for added support.
  ◆ *Active Experimentation*: Observation and Feedback Loop to try out administration.

◆ **Learn about Socratic Seminars.**
  ◆ *Reflective Observation*: Classroom Visitation to see it implemented with students.
  ◆ *Abstract Conceptualization*: Teacher Study Group to study its effectiveness.
  ◆ *Active Experimentation*: Observation and Feedback Loop to try it in classroom.
  ◆ *Concrete Experience*: Lesson Study to refine its implementation.

Meanwhile, Honey and Mumford's *Typology of Learners* (1982) highlights individual preferences for each stage, which include the theorist, the activist, the reflector, and the pragmatist (Figure 9.1). The value of this surfaces when considering different adult learning styles and ensuring that there are professional learning experiences that appeal to different kinds of learners, but it also acts as a mechanism to transition teachers through varied roles of learning.

Theorists are those who prefer to understand the theory behind innovations and may appreciate learning through faculty workshops, teacher study groups, or lesson study. Those who are activists like to learn by doing and may enjoy engaging in problem solving and group discussions. They will likely favor team meetings, co-planning, and looking at student work

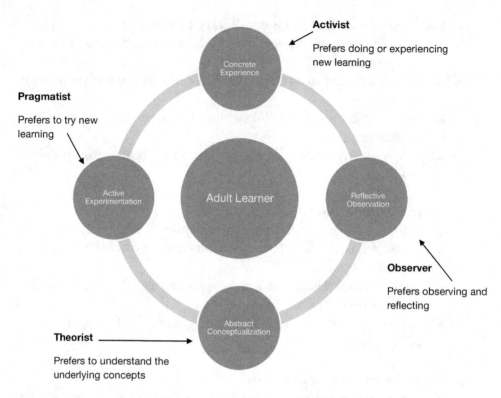

FIGURE 9.1 Honey and Mumford's (1982) Typology of Learners

so that they have the opportunity to collaborate with others. The reflector likes to observe others and gather data before implementing new learning, such as from classroom visitations or modeling. Pragmatists want to see how to implement theory into authentic practice and may benefit from lesson study, observation and feedback loops, and coaching cycles. Taken together, these learning theories lay the framework for planning a cohesive professional development plan.

How Is a Focus for Professional Development Identified?

School districts provide the average teacher 68 hours of professional development a year at a cost of 18 billion dollars annually, but a study conducted by the Boston Consulting Group revealed that nearly one in five never had a voice in their professional development. Those teachers who did have autonomy in what they learned expressed more than twice the level of satisfaction with professional development over those with less choice (The Bill and Melinda Gates Foundation, 2014). This desire to have an active voice and control over one's own learning is one of the tenets of andragogy that greatly enhances participant desire for professional development—to be present, to learn, and to implement new knowledge.

Although a significant focus of professional development typically arises from school system initiatives in which all schools within that district play a part in enacting, other learning emerges from school-based choices developed from the needs identified by the leadership team or, most appealing to teachers, derived by the identified requests of teachers themselves. It may be inescapable to avoid initiatives established at the school system level or even school level, but literacy coaches can tailor professional learning experiences to address individual learning needs.

Collecting data from a needs survey produces robust information about what individual teachers already know, what they are interested in learning more about, and what patterns materialize as to the competencies and needs of the entire school faculty (Stover et al., 2011). For example, if an administrator and leadership team elect to focus on increasing academic rigor, the literacy coach may lead some introductory workshop sessions on what defines rigor, what it looks like in classrooms, and how to adjust instruction to ensure that all students experience raises in academic rigor—regardless of their age, existing skill sets, or content capabilities. To differentiate additional learning experiences, the literacy coach may then prepare a needs survey, such as the one illustrated in Table 9.2.

Based on the needs of the school, the literacy coach may focus school wide on the topics most selected by faculty members or use the results to

TABLE 9.2 Differentiating Professional Development Needs Survey

Which of the following topics would you like to focus on during our work on increasing the academic rigor of classroom instruction? Please check all in which you are interested.

Increasing Academic Rigor
Topics

Leveraging Content Standards to Increase Cognitive Rigor

Using Questioning to Elevate Student Thinking

Promoting Text-Dependent Student Discussions

Increasing Rigor Through Complex Texts

Supporting Struggling Students Through Academically Rigorous Tasks

Making Student Engagement a Partner in Academic Rigor

Aligning Rigorous Instruction with Cognitively Challenging Assessments plan differentiated professional development opportunities for grade levels or individual teachers. This tactic incorporates teacher choice and autonomy as well as cultivating a professional learning culture that encourages ongoing improvement.

On a broader scale, professional development plans may benefit from a needs survey that looks at instruction in a more comprehensive manner and emphasizes best practices. Table 9.3 (also found in Appendix B) suggests a sample from an elementary school that systematically identifies priority needs.

This same strategy can be equally valuable in secondary school settings (Table 9.4 and Appendix B) with a slightly different focus that can engage not only literacy teachers but also teachers from other content areas.

This information provides corroborating evidence in tandem with student achievement data for designing a targeted professional development plan that addresses the unique needs of an individual school, its faculty members, and its students.

TABLE 9.3 Elementary School Needs Survey

Please note the three topics that would most enhance your instructional skills. They may include a literacy focus, content area study, or instructional strategies.

Reading
___ Phonological awareness
___ Decoding skills
___ Morphology (prefixes, roots, and suffixes)
___ Vocabulary development
___ Comprehensive strategies

Writing
___ Building sentences
___ Constructing paragraphs
___ Grammar and mechanics
___ Narrative writing
___ Informative/explanatory writing
___ Opinion writing

Speaking & Listening
___ Collaborative discussions
___ Active listening
___ Student presentations

Instructional Planning
___ Using data to drive instruction
___ Lesson planning
___ Unit planning
___ Student engagement
___ Crafting instruction

Building an Instructional Repertoire
___ Differentiation
___ Critical thinking
___ Instructional rigor
___ Classroom management
___ Struggling learners
___ English language learners

Content Area Study
___ Content area reading
___ Taking notes
___ Study Skills

TABLE 9.4 Secondary School Needs Survey

Please check which areas of professional development are your priority for instructional improvement during the upcoming academic year.

Interactive Learning Strategies	**Best Practices**
___ Pre-Reading	___ Student Engagement
___ During Reading	___ Classroom Management
___ Post-Reading	___ Critical Thinking
___ Vocabulary	___ Academic Rigor
___ Writing Across the Disciplines	___ Differentiation
Diverse Learners	**Assessment**
___ At-Risk Students	___ Authentic Assessment Tools
___ Struggling Readers	___ Developing Student Rubrics
___ Students with Special Needs	___ Constructing Quality Assessments
___ Disengaged Learners	___ Interpreting Assessment Results
___ English Language Learners	___ Data-Driven Instruction

What Forms Can Professional Learning Take?

Joyce and Showers (2002) suggest that teachers require 20 separate experiences with new learning in order to incorporate it fully into their own practice—and this number may increase if the new learning is particularly complex or sophisticated. While this may seem extreme, Fullan (2001) cautions about the "implementation dip" in which teachers engage with new learning but fail to implement it. This is one explanation for why the stand-alone workshop approach to professional development has proven so ineffective. Teachers need additional time and support to embed new learning into teaching practice.

Without finding success in implementing new learning, teachers tend to revert back to past practice—even if it has been ineffective. To counter this outcome, literacy coaches must remain vigilant in strengthening their classroom colleagues' implementation of new practice, providing ongoing support, and reflecting on how best to pair introductory workshops with ongoing classroom-embedded coaching or other learning combinations that allow teachers to learn in different formats and contexts, such as through discussions, modeling, co-teaching, and classroom visits (Gulamhussein, 2013).

Faculty Workshops

It may appear to be a disservice to provide a one-size-fits-all workshop, but it is the most used form of professional development in most school systems. It can also be an efficient method for introductory sessions where all faculty members need to build a preliminary knowledge base of new pedagogy or content knowledge. Whatever the purpose, teachers value workshops that are relevant to their classrooms, address the needs of their own students, and offer the potential for immediate implementation. In other words—Will this help me be better at my work? Will it help my students? How can I use it? Those three questions should drive the planning and delivery of workshop sessions.

Team Meetings

A less formal type of professional development is the team meeting. This time when grade-level or content area teachers come together to collaborate presents a powerful opportunity to personalize learning. The literacy coach can lead the meeting or act as a participant and be more of a resource partner. If the role of leader is taken, however, there should be an explicit focus that unmistakably links to student achievement. While this may seem like less intensive professional learning, Mizell (2010) argues that teachers working collaboratively to problem solve about student needs comprise the most effective professional learning.

Classroom Visitations

The literacy coach may arrange for teachers to visit their colleagues' classrooms in order to observe others' practice as a means to refine their own pedagogy. This form of professional development creates a cadre of confident teachers within a professional learning community as well as augments the school's professional culture in two distinct ways: the teacher whose classroom is being observed demonstrates high-quality instruction and shares the expertise that exists within the school while the visiting teacher(s) learn from colleagues and come to understand that collaboration is a natural process in professional learning and growth.

When conducting a classroom visitation, the literacy coach should adhere to a six-step course of action (Figure 9.2). At the onset, there should be a clearly stated purpose for the classroom visitation. A visitation typically takes place as a means for a classroom teacher to see a particular practice in the classroom with real students so that theory becomes authentic action. With the purpose identified, the literacy coach needs to locate a teacher in the school that demonstrates skillful instructional practice and obtains

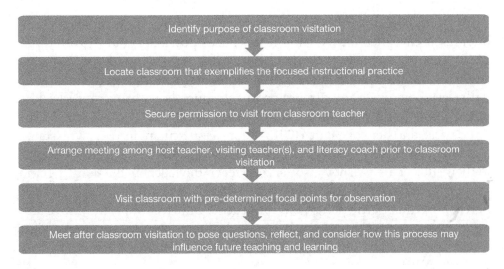

FIGURE 9.2 Six Steps for Classroom Visitations

permission to come and observe. Before the actual visit, the visited and visiting teacher(s) along with the literacy coach should pre-conference in order to clarify the purpose and how data will be collected. Grimm, Kaufman, and Doty (2014) suggest three particular methods: 1) scripting the teacher and students, 2) counting specific elements of the lesson (e.g., the number of questions asked at different levels of Bloom's Taxonomy or Webb's DOK levels), and 3) tracking aspects of the classroom to identify patterns or trends (e.g., the number of students who responded to questions without being called on by the teacher). With this data in hand, the literacy coach arranges a post-visitation conference to allow everyone involved to pose questions, reflect on implications on teaching and learning, and plan concrete steps for how the visiting teacher may modify practice based on this process.

Teacher Study Groups

The concept of Teacher Study Groups (TSGs) appeared in professional literature over three decades ago (Sugai, 1983) and supports sustained, collaborative professional learning in three important areas—innovations in curriculum and instructional practices, school improvement collaboration, and evidence-based research on teaching and learning (Murphy, 1992). Despite its potential to enhance instructional improvement, it is still a relatively underused tool in most schools.

Teacher Study Groups may be shaped by shared interest in a given topic and involve accessing books, articles, or videos and then engaging in collaborative conversations about how it might influence their own practice

(Allington, 2001) or a more focused approach in which participants do their own research, collecting as many resources as possible about a given topic. TSGs may also concentrate on a particular strategy with professional study followed by actually trying out the strategy in their own classrooms with classroom visits and discussion to determine how to improve their use of the strategy (Cayuso, Fegan, & McAlister, 2013).

Cayuso and her colleagues (2013) quote a participant in TSGs who stated that study groups "guide the teachers into doing more research that pertains to their subject areas. They also serve to teach the teachers the 'why' behind some of the requirements we place on them" (p. 1). Beyond the positive perceptions that participants hold for Teacher Study Groups, they have also demonstrated positive effects in research, including teacher knowledge, teacher practice, and student outcomes (Gersten, Dimino, Jayanthi, Kim, & Santoro, 2010).

For a literacy coach who would like to incorporate Teacher Study Groups, several guidelines should be followed, including limiting the group to six to twelve members, establishing norms and expectations during the initial meeting, and expecting collective responsibility for preparing for meetings and contributing to the discussion. For materials to be read or viewed, ensure that the members have the materials prior to the meeting with an agreed-upon timeline for readings, discussions, and any outside tasks (e.g., trying a strategy in their own classrooms).

Observation and Feedback Loop

As a means to monitor instructional implementation, the observation and feedback loop offers one of the most powerful tools at a literacy coach's disposal. Observation creates the opportunity for an objective "eye" to visit a teacher and focus on how students learn in the classroom. Although there should always be a specific instructional focus and corresponding questions to guide the observation, there are some customary inquiries that can structure an initial conversation.

- ◆ What is the focus of this lesson?
- ◆ What is your objective in teaching this lesson?
- ◆ What do you want students to be able to do independently after completing this lesson?
- ◆ How does this lesson fit into a unit/school focus/district initiative?
- ◆ What aspect of the lesson do you think might be challenging for students? How are you planning to address it?
- ◆ How is the lesson differentiated for diverse learners?

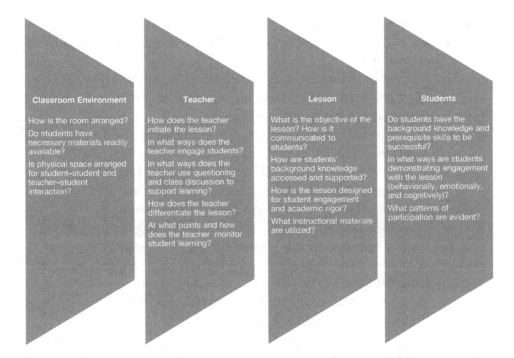

FIGURE 9.3 Observation Framework

Along with these preliminary questions, an observational framework that scrutinizes classroom environment, lesson design, teacher actions, and student interactions and responses provides for multifaceted analysis and subsequent constructive conversations after the observation (Figure 9.3). Noting elements about all four allows a literacy coach to garner a basic sense of teaching and learning in a particular classroom. Selecting only one aspect, such as the lesson, provides greater insight into how one particular dimension of the classroom is influencing student outcomes. However the literacy coach utilizes the framework, observation should always be undertaken for the purpose of gleaning how experiences in the classroom are shaping student learning and in what ways learning can be enhanced.

Student work should be at the heart of a post-conference debriefing, furthering reflective practice and targeting a specific instructional goal. Questions can cover a range of teaching and learning topics, depending on the goal of the observation and feedback loop for a given teacher. They may be used as a means to set the stage for contemplating how the lesson was designed, as an opportunity to examine student work, as a lens to consider student engagement, or as a lever for future planning. The questions below can open a dialogue to these purposes.

- ◆ **Analyze lesson design.**
    - ◆ What was the instructional objective you were trying to accomplish?
    - ◆ Did the objective align to the content standards? How so?
    - ◆ Were instructional materials/manipulatives used in the lesson? How did they influence student learning?
    - ◆ How did you solve problems encountered along the way (e.g., attending to tasks, misbehavior, lack of understanding)?
    - ◆ Was instruction scaffolded to support student learning?
    - ◆ How were students grouped for the lesson? How did the grouping configuration influence student learning?
    - ◆ How was student learning monitored throughout the lesson?
    - ◆ What went well with the lesson? How do you know?
    - ◆ Were there any difficulties with the lesson? How do you know? How did you address them?
    - ◆ Was the objective met for all students? How so?
    - ◆ What have you learned from this lesson?

- ◆ **Examine student work.**
    - ◆ What does the student work tell us about learning?
    - ◆ Did the students learn what you hoped that they would learn based on the objective of the lesson? How do you know?

- ◆ **Discuss student engagement and understanding of the lesson.**
    - ◆ Were students engaged behaviorally? How do you know?
    - ◆ Were students engaged emotionally? How do you know?
    - ◆ Were students engaged cognitively? How do you know?
    - ◆ In what ways did students demonstrate their understanding of the lesson?
    - ◆ Did any students exhibit difficulty with the lesson? Why might that be? How did you address it?

- ◆ **Plan next steps for future instruction.**
    - ◆ What did today's lesson suggest to you about future instruction?
    - ◆ What aspects of the lesson, or future lessons, might you adjust to meet the needs of your students?

Observation, however, is merely the first step. "The main reason to conduct classroom observations is to generate actionable feedback for improving practice" (Kane, 2012, p. 40). After reviewing over 8,000 studies on feedback,

John Hattie (1992) made the argument that "the most powerful single modification that enhances achievement is feedback. The simplest prescription for improving education must be 'dollops of feedback'" (p. 9). In 2007, Hattie and his colleague, Helen Timperly, recommended three essential feedback questions that coaches can use to guide feedback and their work with classroom teachers. Where am I going? (What are my goals?) How am I going? (What progress am I making?) Where to next? (How can I support better progress?) They suggest that "these three questions address the dimensions of feed up, feedback, and feed forward" (p. 88).

They also identified four levels of feedback, with each successive level becoming more effective in its ability to improve performance: feedback about the self on a personal level (FS), feedback about the task (FT), feedback about processing the task (FP), and feedback about self-regulation (FR). Personal feedback (FS) offers evaluations about the individual that "contains little task-related information and is rarely converted into more engagement, commitment to learning goals, enhanced self-efficacy, or understanding about the task" (p. 96). It may, however, be useful for providing emotional support for a novice or struggling teacher. Feedback about the task (FT) concentrates on how well a task is being achieved and may place a spotlight on the immediate goal but not the instructional thinking and planning to attain the goal. Feedback about the task moves to a more instructional focus, but it constricts learning to only that task and is typically not generalizeable to other tasks. It gains strength, however, if it focuses on inaccurate hypotheses or ideas and leads the teacher to consider alternative thinking. Feedback about processing the task (FP) emphasizes the processing, or thinking, at the core of the task as well as how to extend the task and is the most helpful when the teacher uses the feedback to search for other strategies that may be more effective. Taken together, feedback about the task and the processing required to complete the task can strengthen both the initial task as well as future tasks and strategy implementation. The most powerful form of feedback is one in which the teachers transitions from task, to processing, and then to self-regulation. Feedback about self-regulation (FR) is effective in that it requires a level of autonomy and self-direction not visible in the other feedback levels.

Within the context of a literacy coach's observation and feedback cycle, personal feedback may boost confidence or build an affable relationship with a colleague, but it will rarely move instructional practice. Feedback about a task can be insightful within a specific lesson, but literacy coaches can often find themselves returning to this level of feedback over and over again. This can be problematic as it looks at the surface of the lesson without drawing the classroom teachers' attention to the thinking behind how the lesson was developed or how the outcome of the lesson may influence future instruction. Thus, observation and feedback provides greater support at the feedback on processing level in which literacy coaches and classroom teachers actively engage with thinking about instruction at a deeper, more reflective degree. Feedback about self-regulation requires time and commitment but supports the notion that classroom teachers will reflect in conjunction with their literacy coach to contemplate how their instruction influences student learning.

Modeling

Classroom teachers commonly ask literacy coaches to model lessons, current strategies, or aspects of new school initiatives. Demonstrating a lesson in a classroom offers several advantages to the coaching process: it substantiates the coach's teaching skills and willingness to work alongside classroom colleagues; it makes issues about teaching and learning evident in ways that may not be readily apparent within pedagogical theory or instructional materials; and it scaffolds professional learning.

Scaffold professional learning. This caveat is central to the effectiveness of modeling to enhance instructional improvement in meaningful ways. Modeling can become a one-time event with no connection to a classroom teacher's long-term goals for professional learning, with literacy coaches often voicing the concern that they model repeatedly with no change in instructional practice. To remedy this problem, the literacy coach should link modeling to a broader learning goal for the classroom teacher. While occasionally modeling may be isolated and only require one demonstration (e.g., modeling how to implement a simple strategy), a standard for coaching practice should be to embed modeling as another facet of a more

TABLE 9.5 Planning Worksheet for Modeling in the Classroom

Modeling Objective _____

Modeled Lesson/Strategy _____

Guiding Questions
◆ What will the teacher be doing while the lesson /strategy is being modeled (e.g., scripting, taking notes, tracking student behaviors)?
◆ What will the teacher be able to do after observing this lesson/strategy?
◆ In what ways will modeling influence student learning?
◆ How will professional learning be sustained after modeling (e.g., professional dialogue, co-planning, teacher observation and feedback loop)?

comprehensive coaching process with set objectives and expected outcomes. Using a planning worksheet increases clarity and facilitates meaningful dialogue (see Table 9.5 and Appendix B).

Co-Planning

Another dimension of coaching is co-planning with classroom colleagues. Some classroom teachers benefit from using co-planning as a launch for collaborative work in the classroom though modeling or co-teaching; others profit from working with a literacy coach to think through the planning and delivery of instruction but do not require regular classroom visits. In either context, co-planning can often be more effective than modeling as observing another educator in the classroom does not necessarily demonstrate how the lesson was designed, subtle nuances in content delivery or student interactions, or how to replicate that instruction in the future. Co-planning, on the other hand, directs attention to the "why" and "how" of teaching and advances the classroom teacher's own professional understanding and repertoire.

Co-Teaching

Shared responsibility characterizes the effects of co-teaching. It requires the literacy coach and the classroom teacher to plan together, teach side by side, observe one another, and maintain consistent, ongoing dialogue about their teaching practices and the resulting student outcomes. Co-teaching is particularly valuable when teachers may be unwilling to try something by themselves, when having another educator with a different skill set or pedagogical approach may lend insight into student learning, or when the experience of co-teaching can lead to deeper professional dialogue and learning.

A caution for literacy coaches here is that co-teaching is a transitory stage. As with all of the other forms of professional learning described in this chapter, it should follow a gradual release of responsibility. For example, coaching may begin with modeling ("I do"), but it should transition to co-teaching ("we do"), and then move back to the classroom teacher's responsibility with the observation and feedback loop ("you do").

Lesson Study

This form of professional learning originated in Japan with educators in that country seeking to examine their own practice and improve instruction for their students. The term lesson study comes from the Japanese word *jugyokenkyu* and is an inquiry-based model of professional development that involves groups of teachers acting in concert to develop, teach, and improve lessons with "observation of live classroom lessons by a group of teachers who collect data on teaching and learning and collaboratively analyze it" (Lewis, Perry, & Friedkin, 2009, p. 143).

Lesson study has been lauded by teachers in the United States for its attributes of teacher ownership and student-centered focus (Armstrong, 2011) and is considered the highest form of professional learning in Japan (Lewis, 2000). Significantly, in Hanford's (2015) review of lesson study, she quotes educational researcher James Hiebert who makes the argument that "everything we do in the U.S. is focused on the effectiveness of the individual. Is this teacher effective? Not, are the methods they're using effective, and could they use other methods?" (n.p.) and goes on to make the case that if education is to improve "we need to shift from thinking about how to improve *teachers* to thinking about how to improve *teaching*. Lesson study is one way to do that" (n.p.). Lesson study, then, reinforces the mindset that literacy coaching doesn't focus on individual teachers and any perceived strength or weakness; rather, the focal point remains on student learning and how the act of teaching is continually modified based on new pedagogical learning and student need. This idea is highlighted in Lewis and Hurd's (2011) book, *Lesson Study Step by Step: How Teacher Learning Communities Improve Instruction*, in which they quote a first-year teacher's reaction to lesson study: "In the United States, if you are being observed, it's a critique of you. Lesson study focuses on student learning. . . . It takes what we're doing to a more professional level" (p. 36).

Initiating lesson study requires participants to view teaching through a lens of inquiry and ongoing learning with a willingness to be much more actively engaged than in traditional forms of professional development. Membership is generally limited to six members, and prior to beginning the work of lesson study members should set group norms and develop a schedule for meetings. With logistics decided, the group shifts its attention to the topic to be studied (e.g., explanatory writing, determining importance in text, vocabulary development, citing textual evidence, differentiated practices). The structure of lesson study itself is built on a research question stemming from an identified student need within that topic as group members review current research on the topic as well as their own current practice with a common progression being to plan jointly a "research lesson" with one teacher agreeing to teach the lesson while the others observe and collect data, such as through video recording, observational notes, and student work samples. During the post-lesson meeting, they debrief about strengths and weaknesses they observed as well as challenges in its

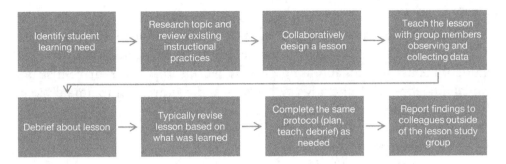

FIGURE 9.4 Lesson Study Progression

implementation in the classroom—all pivoting on the evidence of student learning. Often, the lesson is revised and then re-taught in another classroom while other teachers again observe, followed by another debriefing. At the conclusion of their work together, they report to colleagues outside their lesson study group an answer to their research question and share what they have learned from the process (see Figure 9.4).

Looking at Student Work

While lesson study focuses on instructional design, Looking at Student Work (LASW) concentrates on student products. Both are carried out through a stance of investigation and analysis, but "focusing teacher dialogue on real artifacts can surface tacit differences in our expectations and teaching practices" (Goodwin & Hein, 2016, p. 79). This conviction was reiterated by Windschitl, Thompson, and Braaten (2011) who cautioned that the benefits of this process hinged on whether LASW members viewed analyzing student work in the context of "puzzles of practice" and not "problems with students."

A LASW team may have between four and twelve members (if there is enough time for everyone to contribute) and typically requires 45–60 minutes of dedicated time. The team includes a facilitator to support the group's thinking who re-focuses them if members stray from the work at hand and manages the time constraints. A presenter is responsible for bringing student work samples (with student names removed to eliminate subjectivity) and scoring rubrics as well as sharing the context in which the work took place. LASW teams often use standard protocols to guide their work together.

LASW protocols are helpful in structuring thinking and discussion about student work. They can also make conversations about student work samples less threatening to participants by following a pre-set agenda; thus, no one who brings their own student work samples should feel singled out or criticized. One of the most common is the Tuning Protocol (Blythe, Allen, & Powell, 1999), which is useful for calibrating teacher grading, analyzing student needs, and collaborating on how work samples can drive instructional adjustments. It includes eight steps and requires approximately one hour to complete.

1. Introduction (5 minutes).
2. Presentation of Student Work (10–15 minutes).
3. Clarifying Questions (3–5 minutes).
4. Examining the Work (10–15 minutes).
5. Pause for Silent Reflection on Warm (Supportive) and Cool (Challenging) Feedback (2–3 minutes).
6. Warm and Cool Feedback (10–15 minutes).
7. Reflection (3–5 minutes).
8. Debrief (3–5 minutes).

The Coalition of Essential Schools and the Annenberg Institute for School Reform originally developed a process to bring teachers together about a particular dilemma and help them see the problem more clearly as well as to contemplate how to resolve it. Originally termed the Consultancy Protocol (Dunne, Evans, & Thompson-Grove, n.d.), the National School Reform Faculty (n.d.) adapted it for the purpose of examining student work. In their version, the protocol requires both a presenter who shares a dilemma involving student work and a facilitator for the group. They suggest at least 60 minutes to complete this work.

1. Presenter shares overview of the student work (5 minutes).
2. Group examines student work (5 minutes).
3. Group poses clarifying questions to the presenter (5 minutes).
4. Group poses probing questions to the presenter (10 minutes).
5. Group discusses dilemma without comments by the presenter; presenter listens and takes notes (15 minutes).
6. Presenter responds to group discussion; possible whole-group discussion might take place if time allows (10 minutes).
7. Facilitator discusses group's observation of the protocol (10 minutes).

Protocols, however, can also be restrictive and too formal for some situations. Another issue for many schools is the lack of time available to complete a LASW protocol as most require approximately an hour. For a more

TABLE 9.6 LASW Guided Analysis and Reflection

Before Reviewing Student Work	While Reviewing Student Work	After Reviewing Student Work
◆ What standard is being addressed in this work sample? ◆ Where does this work sample fall within the instructional sequence? What has already been taught? What will be taught after this work sample? ◆ What is deemed "proficient" for this work? Did the student(s) know these expectations? ◆ How long did the student(s) work on this assignment?	◆ How does this work meet/ not meet the standards? ◆ What does this work tell us about what the student(s) understands? ◆ What strengths does the work demonstrate? ◆ What deficits does the work show? ◆ Do any patterns emerge about student thinking and learning? ◆ What instruction might support students from the point they are currently?	◆ What did you discover about student learning based on this process? ◆ What insights did you gain from your colleagues? ◆ Did you see or hear anything today that was surprising or intriguing? ◆ How might you adjust your instruction in reaction to what you learned today? ◆ Did this process raise any questions about teaching and learning for you?

spontaneous conversation with less time commitment, Table 9.6 includes questions that can guide conversation when meeting with classroom teachers.

Examining Achievement Data

Students are tested regularly, but the data generated is only useful if it influences instructional practices in the classroom; achievement data must be a living entity with which administrators, literacy coaches, and classroom teachers engage in ongoing dialogue and not a dead document that resides in a filing cabinet that is never reviewed or discussed. While the literacy coach's role as a data analyst was discussed previously, the power of data resurfaces here as a form of professional development. Examining achievement data (classroom, interim, and annual) should be systematically and intentionally included as a tool to make instructional decisions (Hamilton, Halverson, Jackson, Mandinach, Supovitz, & Wayman, 2009). If it is important enough to test students, then it has power to induce instructional improvement. Below is a list of guiding questions for a data analysis protocol that channels professional inquiry into data, instructional practices, and identified needs.

1. What areas of student performance are at or above expectations?
2. What areas of student performance are below expectations?
3. How did various groups (e.g. gender, race, socioeconomic, disability, English proficiency) of students perform?
4. What are other data telling us about student performance in this area?
5. What confirms what we already know? What challenges what we thought?
6. What important observations seem to "pop out" from the data? Surprising observations? Unexpected observations?
7. What patterns or trends appear?
8. What similarities and differences exist across various data sources?
9. What do we observe at the school level? The grade level? The class level?
10. What are some things we have not yet explored? What other data do we want to examine?

(Killion, 2008, p. 8)

Data discussions should be incorporated as a consistent use of professional learning time with structures in place to review and analyze data as a tool to improve student learning (U.S. Department of Education, 2009). Used in tandem with other forms of professional development, they build a culture of inquiry, analysis, and reflective practice that supports high-quality instruction and positive student learning outcomes.

Coaching Cycles

Of all of the forms of professional development discussed in this chapter, coaching cycles are the most frequently associated with what classroom teachers view as "literacy coach work" in schools and are generally well perceived as being effective (Gross, 2010). Neufeld and Roper (2003) argue that "when coaching is integral to a larger instructional improvement plan that targets and aligns professional development resources toward the district's goals, it has the potential to become a powerful vehicle for improving instruction and, thereby, student achievement" (p. 26).

Although there are variations, the coaching cycle commonly follows a three-step observational protocol of pre-conference, observation, and post-conference (Garmston, Linder, & Whitaker, 1993; Robbins, 2015). Jim Knight and his colleagues (2015) classify those stages as identify, learn, and improve. Some models suggest that the cycle rests solely on modeling and observation, but alternatives exists in which the literacy coach and classroom teacher can follow one of three pathways.

1. The classroom teacher models a lesson followed by a debriefing with feedback by the literacy coach.
2. The classroom teacher and literacy coach co-plan and co-teach a lesson with a subsequent debriefing with paired reflection.
3. The literacy coach models a lesson followed by a debriefing and feedback by the classroom teacher.

The choice should be based on shared decision making by the literacy coach and classroom teacher as to which option best supports the identified student learning goal and coaching goal. It may also transition as collaboration continues. For example, the coaching cycle may begin with the literacy coach modeling a lesson and then transition to the classroom teacher.

While comparable to the observation and feedback loop and sometimes used synonymously, the coaching cycle tends to be more time intensive, more rigorous, and cyclical in nature with recurring collaboration. An observation and feedback loop may consist of only one rotation and be completed within a week (this sometimes comes about when an administrator requests the literacy coach to observe a teacher for a particular purpose); however, a literacy coach typically devotes from two to six weeks to a coaching cycle. The exact length depends on the complexity of the instructional practice, the skill set of the classroom teacher, and the frequency with which the literacy coach and classroom teacher can meet.

The coaching cycle begins with a pre-conference as a means to identify the coaching goal, learn about teacher expectations, and organize logistics for collaborating. Table 9.7 (also found in Appendix B) provides a pre-conference planning sheet to direct the conversation and facilitate planning.

With this information in hand, the focus shifts to the classroom, and a lesson is taught (by the literacy coach, the teacher, or jointly). In either scenario, observational notes should be taken to aid in more focused observation and richer discussion during the debriefing. A framework for this can be helpful in organizing these observational notes (see Table 9.8 and Appendix B).

The post-conference can take three forms: mirroring, collaborative, or expert. The mirroring post-conference requires the least time and interaction between the teacher and coach, focusing on simply providing evidence of a particular practice (e.g., script, recording of the lesson, or an instrument designed to gather information about the teacher-selected focus) to the instructor with no dialogue or shared reflection of the lesson. The collaborative post-conference engages both classroom teacher and literacy coach in a reflection about the lesson. In the expert post-conference, the literacy coach

TABLE 9.7 Pre-Conferencing Planning Sheet

Pre-Conference Planning Sheet	
Teacher's Name: Grade Level: Content Area:	Length of Coaching Cycle:
Student-Learning Goal:	Notes:
Coaching Goal:	Notes:
Scheduling for Classroom Visits:	Scheduling for Debriefs:
Literacy Coach Responsibilities:	Classroom Teacher Responsibilities:
Student Work Products/Assessments to Be Collected as Evidence of Effective Practice:	
Confirming Evidence That Coaching Cycle Has Reached Its Goal:	

TABLE 9.8 Observational Notes

Observational Notes	
Instructor's Name:	Date:
Coaching Goal:	Lesson Focus:
What the Instructor Said:	What the Instructor Did:
How the Students Responded:	Evidence of Student Learning:
Additional Notes:	

takes on the role of an authority providing instruction to the teacher both in the pre-conference as well as in the post-conference, leading the teacher in the reflection as well as in future practice (Robbins, 2015). While time constraints sometimes compel literacy coaches to fall back on the mirroring post-conference, much greater reflection and professional learning takes place with either the collaborative or expert post-conference. Using a post-conference recording form can also be an effective tool for leveraging the observation into influencing teacher practice (see Table 9.9 and Appendix B) and as a tool to "cycle" back to a new pre-conference, observation, and post-conference rotation built on what has been learned.

Coaching cycles offer the promise of collaborative relationships, professional inquiry and growth, and increased gains in student achievement. They should not be considered as an isolated activity that begins and ends with

TABLE 9.9 Post-Conference Recording Form

Post-Conference Recording Form	
Teacher Name: Grade/Content Area: Date:	
Lesson Focus:	*How did the lesson go? Were students successful? Based on what evidence?*
Student Learning Goal:	*Was the goal met? Based on what evidence?*
Coaching Goal:	*Was the goal met? Based on what evidence?*
What are your next steps?	*How can I support you?*
Additional Notes:	

no real change in future practice. Rather, coaching cycles provide classroom teachers the grounds for an action plan for instructional improvement.

How Can Coaching Be Equitable for All Teachers?

A startling fact revealed by the Boston Consulting Group study funded by the Bill and Melanie Gates Foundation (2014) was the negative perception teachers in their research held regarding coaching. Their reasoning, how-ever, exposes an often neglected dilemma in the field of coaching. Only half of the participants in the study had received coaching in the previous 12 months, and for those teachers the level of collaboration differed widely with 57 percent receiving either weekly or monthly sessions. Why? Principals in the same study disclosed that they directed their coaches to work with new and struggling teachers 60 percent of the time. Classroom teachers don't want sporadic coaching; they are looking for ongoing, consistent support, yet Figure 9.5 demonstrates how coaching may appear in some schools.

Too often administrators designate the majority of a literacy coach's time to support only a few teachers, leaving the rest of the faculty with little to no professional development support and effectively reducing the coaching process to a triage mentality of survival with little time for classroom teachers who would benefit from enhancing their own skill set. Importantly, ignoring these teachers limits the potential of increasing achievement for large numbers of students; also, more expert teachers often share new learning with their colleagues in a way that amplifies professional improvement and growth. Consequently, the danger of this practice is that by focusing so heavily on such a small number of teachers, the professional "health" of the

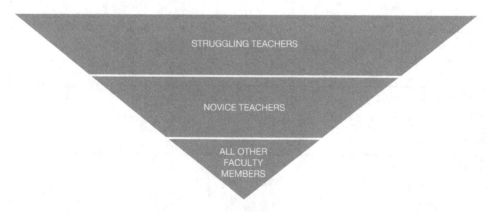

FIGURE 9.5 Literacy Coaching Reality in an "Unhealthy" School

entire school is compromised. While it is critical that literacy coaches work with those who need immediate, critical support, to do so to the detriment of other teachers negatively influences the professional culture of the school, the achievement of its students and, ultimately, how the role of the literacy coach is recognized. When working almost exclusively with teachers who struggle, the perception becomes not one of shared inquiry and ongoing learning and growth but one that only under-performing teachers work with the literacy coach. That is a dangerous assessment and threatens the viability of a literacy coach to build relationships or partner with classroom colleagues.

Coaching Rotations for All Faculty Members

An alternative to the inverted triangle is an innovative approach to literacy coaching. It also involves three tiers, but these tiers are arranged hierarchically as a means to enhance professional learning for all faculty members (see Figure 9.6). In this model, the majority of the literacy coach's time is devoted to the faculty as a whole, utilizing rotations to reach teachers at all grades and content areas. For example, the literacy coach would schedule each grade level or content area for a rotation, so that a particular grade or content area would work collaboratively with the literacy coach for a given time. A typical rotation may extend two to six weeks, depending on the complexity of the coaching goal, the individual needs of the teachers, and the frequency with which meetings and classroom visits take place between the literacy coach and the classroom teachers, such as grade one teachers for the month of October or middle school social studies for two weeks in November.

The coaching goal for these rotations would typically be identified based on student data for the entire group but the ways in which teachers in

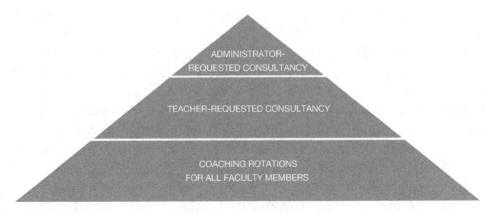

FIGURE 9.6 Multi-Tiered Literacy Coaching in a "Healthy" School

that group access support can be differentiated based on their preferred learning style or instructional need. Thus, a third-grade team may determine vocabulary development as an instructional need based on student data. They may then elect to collaborate throughout the coaching rotation with a teacher study group on current research and best practices for vocabulary instruction, lesson study on using context clues to determine unfamiliar or unknown words, or a coaching cycle on how to use mental imagery to help students build vocabulary concepts. On the other hand, they may ask to work on a more individual basis, with one teacher requesting support in co-planning vocabulary centers for the literacy block, another in co-teaching selected strategies for the entire class, and yet another requesting a one-on-one teacher study group to research vocabulary strategies for English language learners. So, the literacy coach would ensure that they transitioned naturally through the learning stages of acquiring new instructional practices, but how that looks may be greatly differentiated by group and individual teachers.

The scheduled coaching rotation, or even isolated collaborations due to an administrator or classroom teacher request, may also differ on the role for which the classroom teacher needs support—it may not necessarily be in the role of a professional development. It may be a need for a data analyst ("Can you help me examine my students' latest test scores so I can target instruction for my struggling students?"), a resource manager ("I need some information on vocabulary development. Do you have any books or articles that I can read?"), a curriculum expert ("How can I use social studies and science to help my students increase their vocabulary?"), an instructional specialist ("What are some word learning strategies that I could try?"), or as a professional developer ("Would you help me co-plan how I can use my guided reading groups as small-group practice for vocabulary development?").

The purpose, then, is not a one-size-fits-all mentality but an individualized, specialized approach to professional learning. Structuring the work between a literacy coach and a classroom teacher should be jointly determined prior to providing services and monitored to ensure that the goals of coaching are transparent and remain consistent in dialogue and collaboration. Embedded in their work together, the literacy coach should consider the background of the teacher (e.g., novice/experienced and engaged/resistant), the coaching model most beneficial to the unique needs of the teacher (e.g., peer coaching, cognitive coaching, instructional coaching, or content coaching), and resources that may be collected in order to offer this collaboration. Guiding questions can frame collaborating conversations as well as the reflective practice of the literacy coach.

- In what way will this coaching improve student learning outcomes?
- What goal do you have for our collaboration?
- How long will we work together to achieve our goal?
- In what area(s) can I best support your work—data analyst, resources, curriculum, instructional practices, or professional development?
- If you were to focus on professional development, what kind of experience would you prefer (e.g., looking at student work, co-planning, observation and feedback loop)?
- What student artifacts will be collected to determine if our work together is yielding results in your classroom?
- How will we determine if our work together is successful?

This information can also be recorded in a planning worksheet such as the one below (Table 9.10 and Appendix B).

Teacher-Requested Consultancy

The second tier is devoted to classroom teachers who approach the literacy coach for support on their own accord, either for a brief request or for a longer period of engagement. Again, this assistance may take the form of any number of roles that a literacy coach assumes and allows a responsive tactic so that classroom teachers see the literacy coach as offering ongoing support whenever needed.

Administrator-Requested Consultancy

Lastly, the third tier is devoted to those classroom teachers whom administrators direct the literacy coach to assist. There is no doubt that classroom teachers who are struggling merit dedicated, protected time with the literacy coach. They should not, however, appropriate all of the time. A solution to provide equitable support for all faculty members is to set aside a period of time (e.g., 1 to 2 hours weekly) to work with a struggling teacher. This time can be devoted to planning, co-teaching, observation and feedback loop, etc. Struggling teachers would be given added support during their grade-level or content area rotations as well.

Using this multi-tiered approach ensures that coaching is an equitable process for all faculty members. It also allows the literacy coach to organize scheduling and prioritize needs so that the school's professional learning health takes precedence in collaborating with classroom colleagues.

TABLE 9.10 Coaching Planning Worksheet

Teacher's Name: Grade Level: Content Area:			Length of Coaching Cycle:	
Student-Learning Goal:			Notes:	
Coaching Goal:			Notes:	
Coaching Support: Identify the role(s) needed to offer support and how collaboration will take place.				
Data Analyst	Resource Manager	Curriculum Expert	Instructional Specialist	Professional Developer
If professional development is selected, check the form(s) of professional development to be implemented. ◆ Faculty Workshop ◆ Team Meeting ◆ Classroom Visitation ◆ Teacher Study Group ◆ Observation & Feedback Loop ◆ Modeling ◆ Co-Planning ◆ Co-Teaching ◆ Lesson Study ◆ Looking at Student Work ◆ Examining Achievement Data ◆ Coaching Cycle			Notes:	
Student Work Products/Assessments to Be Collected:			Notes:	
Confirming Evidence That Coaching Goal Has Been Met:				

How Can Literacy Coaches Ensure High-Quality Professional Development?

It is important to determine who will receive professional development and what form this learning will take, however the primary goal of professional development is to change practice. That is foremost in all professional development planning, yet teachers often greet professional development sessions with moans and complaints—"Another new initiative! When will we ever use this?" "We have too much work to do in the classroom to take time for this!" "What is the purpose?" "What I do works; why change?" Linda Darling-Hammond and her colleagues found in their 2009 study that 90 percent of teachers attended professional development, but the vast majority of them stated that it wasn't useful with the researchers arguing that reaction stemmed from the pervasive workshop-model approach. In short, teachers can come to view professional development as an act of compliance and not as an opportunity for instructional improvement. When confronted with a reception like this, some literacy coaches become intimidated to present, and others become frustrated with the lack of their classroom colleagues' motivation to participate.

Those who are prepared for this reaction, however, view professional development as one of the most powerful tools in their coaching repertoire to transform the teaching and learning climate of their schools. A reflective, intentional professional developer considers these attitudes and presents an introduction to the work to be done by addressing all of classroom teacher concerns. Participants, then, should come to professional development sessions with a clear understanding of several key facets, which include:

- how this professional development activity aligns to the school's vision,
- the overarching goal of this activity as it links to student learning,
- its specific objectives,
- how it is based on evidence-based practice,
- how research drives its work,
- its expectations for adults,
- how adult learning will be supported,
- how its effectiveness will be measured, and
- the level of its intensity, sustainability, and focus on content.

Coaches aim to transform schools (West & Cameron, 2013) and that requires a vision for how professional development can move the school forward in reaching academic goals for students and collaborating on that vision with faculty members. What's more, the literacy coach must take into account what resources will be necessary and what form professional learning will take to support these goals. One of the most common weaknesses of professional development is the lack of coherency and continuity. To safeguard the effectiveness of the professional development plan, it is important to monitor how adult learning is influencing student learning and provide ongoing assistance in a school culture that is receptive to learning.

In other words, professional development should not be hurriedly cobbled together the day before a scheduled session. Rather, the literacy coach should meet with the administrator and the leadership team and plan the professional development program at least one year in advance. While new initiatives and issues arise that will necessitate adjusting the schedule, it is imperative that there is a focused, purposeful professional development program in place that supports the school's vision and change efforts.

Although there is typically a myriad of issues that need to be addressed to support instructional reform, a skilled literacy coach will settle on one or two significant areas of improvement to center the year's professional development sessions. The literacy coach should also determine how to integrate multiple forms of professional learning experiences to support change in teacher practice. For instance, if a primary goal is to increase student skill with argumentative writing, the professional development plan may include traditional faculty meeting sessions for introductory content but then add collaborative team meetings, coaching cycles, classroom visitations, and looking at student work. By utilizing varying forms of professional learning revolving around the same goal, teachers have multiple opportunities to engage with their own new learning and embrace changes in their practice. Without a plan, however, one of the literacy coach's most powerful tools to improve student performance is lost, and professional development disintegrates into fragmented sessions with little purpose or noticeable change in teacher practice.

What About Working with Students?

Being a literacy coach can be a difficult transition as the professional focus shifts from working with children to working with adults. The mindset and daily practice varies widely between the two, and it can be particularly problematic when administrators or classroom teachers ask if the literacy coach can take students as well. In some school systems, the literacy coach's position entails both aspects; however, if it is not part of the position description the attention should remain on teachers. Otherwise, concentration is lost between two separate goals with less and less time to accomplish either one.

The literacy coach, then, should not work directly with students other than their interaction during demonstration lessons or co-teaching. This may seem uncaring for students who are struggling, but it is necessary to look at the bigger picture in school improvement. Just like the discussion earlier in this chapter about the inverted triangle for coaching adults, if a literacy coach expends time and energy on working with small groups of students then the academic health of the entire school may be jeopardized as fewer faculty members receive support—which, in turn, means fewer students receive enhanced instruction.

Additional Readings on Professional Development

Blythe, T., Allen, D., & Powell, B. S. (2015). *Looking at student work* (3rd ed.). New York, NY: Teachers College Press.

Cayuso, E., Fegan, C., & McAlister, D. (2013). *Designing teacher study groups: A guide for success*. New York, NY: Maupin.

Hattie, J., & Timperley, H. (2007). The power of feedback. *Review of Educational Research, 77*(1), 81–112.

Hurd, J., & Lewis, C. (2011). *Lesson study step by step: How teacher learning communities improve instruction*. Portsmouth, NH: Heinemann.

Love, N., Stiles, K. E., Mundry, S., & DiRanna, K. (2008). *The data coach's guide to improving learning for all students: Unleashing the power of collaborative inquiry*. Thousand Oaks, CA: Corwin.

Martin, L. E., Kragler, S., Quatroche, D. J., & Bauserman, K. L. (2015). *Handbook of professional development in education. Successful models and practices, pre-k-12*. New York, NY: Guilford Press.

PART III

How Does a Coach Ensure Lasting Change?

You cannot force commitment, what you can do . . . you nudge a little here, inspire a little there, and provide a role model. Your primary influence is the environment you create.

Peter Senge

As difficult as it may seem to create change in a school, it is exponentially more difficult to sustain that change over a period of time. It requires more than content knowledge and professional experience. The literacy coach who ensures lasting effects on student achievement must maintain constant vigilance on the school's vision, professional development plan, and student data monitoring.

Beyond that, it will be necessary to be mindful of the human factor. How will teachers who are feeling fatigued from change be supported? What about teachers who believe that the successes they have found mean an end to further change? Some of these concerns can be facilitated by ongoing communication and relationships. Others, however, will necessitate a common commitment to ongoing, purposeful change as a means for consistent school improvement.

This vision for ensuring expert instruction can be further strengthened by reflection. Reflection on the part of administrators. Reflection on the part of classroom teachers. Reflection on the part of the literacy coach. As much as the demands on literacy coaches suggest perpetual movement, sustainability will not take place without quiet, intentional reflection to identify what is working, what isn't, and how the school adapts in order to grow . . . and to thrive.

10

Self-Reflection and Sustaining Change

Follow effective action with quiet reflection; from the quiet reflection will come even more effective action.

Peter Drucker

A common factor linking the varied roles of literacy coaches is that the fundamental characteristic of all of their work revolves around their classroom colleagues. It is their professional responsibility to support the needs of others. While that charge is challenging, it cannot blind literacy coaches to the absolute necessity of reflecting on their own practice. John Dewey once said, "We don't learn from experience. We learn from reflecting on experience." Literacy coaches need self-reflection to explore their own practice as well as the underlying beliefs that guide their work with teachers. This introspection and self-awareness leads to change and greater informed actions (Çimer, Çimer, & Vekli, 2013).

How Does Self-Reflection Sustain Change?

A critical aspect of the partnership literacy coaches maintain with classroom teachers is active inquiry and reflection in professional practice. Literacy coaches ask questions, provide observational feedback, and guide classroom teachers into greater self-discovery and actualization of enhanced teaching and learning experiences. The purpose of these endeavors ultimately lies in the capacity of classroom teachers to engage, eventually, in this high level

> **? COACHING QUESTIONS**
>
> **(for Literacy Coaches)**
>
> 1. What aspects of my work with teachers are working? Why? Can I replicate those efforts for the long term?
> 2. What aspects of my work with teachers are not working? Why not? What can I change about my practice to make my efforts more successful?
> 3. Were the results of my work what I expected? Why or why not?
> 4. Am I reaching my coaching goals? Why or why not?
> 5. How can I be more effective in my goal to increase student achievement?

of reflection without the presence of the coach so that reflective practice becomes engrained into the culture of the school.

These efforts toward greater reflective practice cannot exist without the literacy coach also reflecting. Literacy coaches serve as models for self-reflection but also make use of their contemplation for greater introspection into school improvement efforts, augmenting their capacity to effect sustainable change in the school culture and pedagogical beliefs of their colleagues. Table 10.1 (also found in Appendix B) suggests questions for reflective practice based on coaching rotations.

Self-reflection is simply a non-negotiable in the goal of instructional improvement—for classroom teachers but also, significantly, for literacy coaches. In addition to ongoing reflection, however, is the ability of literacy coaches to continue to update their own instructional skill set. Without a strong pedagogical foundation and continual professional growth, they cannot support the work of others.

Just How Important Are Reading Credentials to a Literacy Coach?

While the field of literacy coaching is filled with classroom teachers who have demonstrated excellent classroom skills and a wealth of literacy knowledge, a basic prerequisite of the position should be reading credentials gained through university-level course work and certification documents issued by state departments of education. Although new literacy coaches can draw upon past professional experiences to help others in the classroom, without a deeper, more comprehensive grasp of literacy principles and

TABLE 10.1 Reflective Practice After a Coaching Rotation

Coaching Process	Guiding Questions for Literacy Coach	Responses
Goals & Objectives	◆ What instructional goal was set for this coaching rotation? ◆ What learning objective was identified for this coaching rotation?	
Actions	◆ In attempting to reach your goal/objective, what went well? ◆ How do you know? ◆ Can you replicate that success with other coaching rotations? ◆ In attempting to reach your goal/objective, what didn't go as well? ◆ How do you know? ◆ What can you change for future coaching rotations?	
Outcomes	◆ Did you reach your goal/objective? ◆ How do you know?	
Feedback	◆ What feedback did you receive from your classroom colleague?	

What have you learned from this process and what aspects of your coaching will you change to improve your practice?

practices they commonly encounter questions and instructional issues that they are simply unprepared to handle. For example, consider an outstanding primary teacher who is given the task of working with teachers in a K-8 building. What experiences does that literacy coach have with middle school curriculum, students, or assessments? Another example comes from a widely respected classroom teacher who has consistently exhibited expert instruction in previous classes but has never been asked to analyze varied forms of data and grapple with determining the implications of student performance data and what instructional practices offer the best course of action for student growth across a range of grade levels and student demographics. Another common problem for classroom teachers with no advanced degree in reading is professional development. This is a common expectation, but many novice literacy coaches—especially those lacking formal training—struggle both with preparing and delivering public presentations.

Are reading credentials really that important? Heineke (2010) studied the issue with the help of four literacy coaches agreeing to become participants in his study. He found that the two coaches who held a master's degree and reading specialist certification experienced much more success in their roles over that of their colleagues who lacked specialized training. Teachers who worked with the credentialed coaches spoke about the coaches' knowledge of literacy and viewed them as beneficial resources for their school, cataloging many of their own instructional practices as being influenced by the work they had completed with their coach. Conversely, those who had worked with non-credentialed literacy coaches expressed positive feelings about their relationship but could identify few instructional practices that had been influenced by their literacy coach.

Developing credibility with faculty members will be difficult if a literacy coach does not have the requisite formal training and certification. Just as other fields in education require specialized training (e.g., school psychologist, speech psychologist, administrator), the field of coaching also demands credentialing if its role in schools is to be deemed valuable and have real import in school improvement efforts.

The importance of reading credentials does not lie simply with the issue of perception and credibility. L'Allier and Elish-Piper (2006) conducted a study that included 5 literacy coaches, 65 K-3 classroom teachers, and 1,596 students. The researchers in this study examined not perceptions but student achievement as they collected fall and spring test scores and weekly literacy coaching logs. Analysis of the data revealed that the highest average student reading gains arose in classrooms supported by a literacy coach with reading credentials. On the other hand, the lowest average student gains appeared in classrooms supported by a literacy coach who lacked certification and formal training.

Thus, those holding positions as literacy coaches without credentials are strongly encouraged to enroll in a university program and begin formal training to ensure their ability to provide the most helpful support to their classroom colleagues. It must also be recognized that while reading credentials may be a prerequisite for skillful coaching, formal training prior to working in the field as a literacy coach is only the beginning. Ongoing professional development is crucial if coaches are to strengthen, refine, and update their professional competency.

How Can Literacy Coaches Continue to Build Their Own Skill Sets?

Some school systems furnish their literacy coaches with professional development so that their abilities in instructional leadership continue to flourish and their schools' change efforts progress in a purposeful, strategic manner. For literacy coaches, however, who find themselves isolated within school systems that fail to offer systematic learning opportunities, they face inadequate professional development (Burkins & Ritchie, 2007).

How can literacy coaches own their learning and continue to develop their knowledge base? First, they need to build off foundations in their own classroom teaching experiences and subsequent certification programs. In addition, professional development while in the field should include the following options.

- Join a professional organization (International Literacy Association).
- Attend professional conferences (International Literacy Association annual conferences in the U.S. and abroad and state conferences).
- Subscribe to professional journals (*The Reading Teacher, The Journal of Adolescent and Adult Literacy, Reading Research Quarterly, Reading and Writing*).
- Network with other literacy coaches and reading experts.
- Stay abreast of current research and trends.
- Conduct action research to determine "what works" in schools and classrooms.

How Can Change Be Sustained?

Even with highly effective literacy coaches who have a wealth of classroom experience, university training, and credentialing, sustaining change can be difficult. As exciting as it is to witness the gains made from developing a vision for change, setting forth an action plan for improvement, and ongoing collaborative efforts of literacy coaches and their classroom colleagues, it can be intimidating to consider not only how to maintain the positive effects created with those initial efforts but also how to nurture future change.

Harrington, Voehl, and Voehl (2014) make the case that "it is one thing to produce a momentary change. It is quite another to sustain the change" (p. 3) and caution that nearly half of all strategic initiatives for changes are unsuccessful. Despite the possibility of a collapse of future positive outcomes, they suggest a model for organizational change that lends itself well to the field of education and the work of literacy coaches. Table 10.2 highlights the steps to be taken to ensure sustainable change and what it looks like in organizations as well as our adaptation for the work of literacy coaches.

As the table demonstrates, the authors originally developed this model for sustaining change for the business world, but these same principles for change management apply equally to the field of education. It begins with

TABLE 10.2 Sustaining Change in Schools

S	◆ *Support from the top*
	◆ Leaders must be responsible and support ongoing improvement efforts
	◆ The leadership team (including principals) must be openly and consistently supporting change effort
U	◆ *Utilize change-sustaining changes*
	◆ Plans for sustaining change efforts must be made
	◆ The school must have a sustainable plan to ensure that disruptions (e.g., changing staff) don't impede efforts
S	◆ *Shift paradigms when needed*
	◆ Plans for ongoing change must communicate benefits of change to help individuals to continue to change
	◆ Be vigilant against inertia and reverting back to what was comfortable and familiar
T	◆ *Talk and communicate*
	◆ Ongoing dialogue is needed to ensure that individuals understand what is expected of them
	◆ Ensure that individuals grasp what and why particular actions, procedures, and behaviors are expected of them
A	◆ *Assimilate and integrate*
	◆ Use change agents to sustain change
	◆ Engage individuals to act as change agents as a means to influence others and as barometers of when change efforts need to increase in intensity
I	◆ *Invest in planning for sustained results*
	◆ As the organization becomes familiar with change, resources can be modified for sustaining change
	◆ Increases in professional capacity and ongoing change efforts produces additional resources for sustaining change
N	◆ *Negotiate results with a portfolio approach*
	◆ Analyze readiness for change before putting strategies in place; adapt as needed
	◆ Embed change efforts into school improvement plan so that an infrastructure is established to facilitate change; organize resources, monitor progress, and be able to articulate

Source: Adapted from Harrington, H. J., Voehl, F., & Voehl, C. F. (2015). *Model for sustainable change* [White paper]. Retrieved from www.pmi.org

ensuring that principals visibly support the literacy coach's efforts. Without leadership from the top, there is little hope for sustainable change. That said, faculty members come and go, so plans must be devised that take into account these shifts in personnel and how transitions may influence change efforts (e.g., How will the literacy coach make certain that all school members are equally prepared to become participants in change efforts?). As time continues, the literacy coach must be aware of the potential for school members to revert back to past practice—what is familiar, comfortable, and less risky. This requires considering what resources and professional development may continue to move the school from what is the present status quo to what is the future goal, which is fostered by making mindset shifts (e.g., What does student achievement suggest about teaching practice? How should teaching practice be adjusted to meet the needs of students? What changes must individuals make to ensure that change happens thoughtfully and consistently?), behavioral changes (e.g., How will classroom instruction look as change is implemented?), and then organizational modifications (e.g., How will administrators support these change efforts? What actions will the literacy coach take? In what ways will success be measured?). This level of change necessitates continued dialogue among school members so that everyone is aware of their roles and responsibilities and searching for other school members who can act as change agents themselves, influencing their colleagues to maintain fidelity to these new innovations as well as making administrators and literacy coaches aware of the progress of change and when modifications need to be made to ensure the sustainability of these changes. With all of these mechanisms in place, individuals become more comfortable with risk-taking and change, professional capacity increases, and the benefits produced naturally transform into school capital that can be re-invested into change efforts. Thus, transformational change becomes cyclical—as one change initiative gains success and sustainability, future change efforts build off of that success and allow the school to continue to grow and flourish.

Final Thoughts

Being a literacy coach is not an easy task. It is challenging, time-consuming, and often daunting in its expectations for significant instructional improvements within schools and individual classrooms. Through the combined efforts of learning the complexity of the varied roles that a literacy coach takes on, honing their own professional practice, and engaging in ongoing self-reflection, literacy coaches have the real opportunity to effect purposeful, meaningful change . . . and sustain it. It isn't easy, but a literacy coach has the possibility to see amazing growth in student achievement and can experience professional rewards unparalleled in education. Plan for change, put intentional actions in motion to make the promise of change possible, continue to reflect on how to improve and sustain change efforts, and then witness just how important a literacy coach can be in the lives of teachers and students.

Additional Readings on Reflection and Sustaining Change

Berry, A. (2008). *Tensions in teaching about teaching: Understanding practice as a teacher educator.* Dordrecht, The Netherlands: Springer.

Holcomb, E. L. (2009). *Asking the right questions: Tools for collaboration and school change.* (3rd ed.). Thousand Oaks, CA: Corwin.

Nolan, J. F. (2007). Five basic principles to facilitate change in schools. *Catalyst for Change, 35*(1), 3–8.

Toll, C. A. (2008). *Surviving but not yet thriving: Essential questions and practical answers for experienced literacy coaches.* Newark, DE: International Reading Association.

York-Barr, J., Sommers, W. A., Ghere, G. S., & Montie, J. (2016). *Reflective practice for renewing schools: An action guide for educators.* Thousand Oaks, CA: Corwin.

References

Alliance for Excellent Education. (2006). *Finding and keeping the teachers we need.* Retrieved from http://all4ed.org/wp-content/uploads/TeacherQualityFactSheet.pdf

Allington, R. (2001). *What really matters for struggling readers.* New York, NY: Maupin House Publishing.

Armstrong, A. (2011). Lesson study puts a collaborative lens on student learning. *Tools for Schools, 14*(4), 1–7. Retrieved from https://www.collaborativeclassroom.org/sites/default/files/media/pdfs/lessonstudy/learning_forward.pdf

Barber, M., & Mourshed, M. (2007). *How the world's best-performing school systems come out on top.* McKinsey and Company. Retrieved from www.smhc-cpre.org/wp-content/uploads/2008/07/how-the-worlds-best-performing-school-systems-come-out-on-top-sept-072.pdf

Bean, R. M. (2009). *The reading specialist: Leadership for the classroom, school and community* (2nd ed.). New York, NY: Guilford Press.

Bean, R. M., Draper, J. A., Hall, V., Vandermolen, J., & Zigmond, N. (2010). Coaches and coaching in Reading First schools: A reality check. *The Elementary School Journal, 111*(1), 87–114.

Bean, R. M., & Eisenberg, E. (2009). Literacy coaching in middle and high schools. In K.D. Wood & W. E. Blanton (Eds.), *Literacy instruction for adolescents: Research-based practice* (pp. 107–124). New York, NY: Guilford Press.

Bean, R. M., Turner, G., Draper, J., Heisey, N., & Zigmond, N. (2008, March). *Coaching and its contributions to reading achievement in Reading First Schools.* Paper presented at the annual meeting of the American Educational Research Association, New York, NY.

Bembry, K. L., Jordan, H. R., Gomez, E., Anderson, M. C., & Mendro, R. L. (1998). *Policy implications of long-term teacher effects on student achievement.* Paper presented at the annual meeting of the American Educational Research Association, San Diego, CA.

Bill and Melinda Gates Foundation (2014). *Teachers know best: Teachers' views on professional development.* Retrieved from https://s3.amazonaws.com/edtech-production/reports/Gates-PDMarketResearch-Dec5.pdf

Bill and Melinda Gates Foundation. (2015). *Teachers know best: Making data work for teachers and students.* Retrieved from http://k12education.gatesfoundation.org/wp-content/uploads/2015/06/TeachersKnowBest-MakingDataWork.compressed.pdf

Blachowicz, C., Obrochta, C., & Fogelberg, E. (2005). Literacy coaching for change. *Educational Leadership*, *62*(6), 55–58.

Blythe, T., Allen, D., & Powell, B. S. (1999). *Looking together at student work*. New York, NY: Teachers College Press.

Boston Public Schools. (1998, March 9). *High school restructuring*. Boston, MA: Author.

Brown, D., Reumann-Moore, R., Hugh, R., Du Plessis, P., & Christman, J. B. (2006). *Promising inroads: Year one report of the Pennsylvania high school coaching initiative*. Philadelphia, PA: Research for Action.

Buly, M. R., Coskie, T., Robinson, L., & Egawa, K. (2006). Literacy coaching: Coming out of the corner. *Voices from the Middle*, *13*(4), 24–28.

Burkins, J., & Ritchie, S. (2007). Coaches coaching coaches. *Journal of Language and Literacy Education*, *3*(1), 32–47.

Bush, R. N. (1984). *Effective staff development in making our schools more effective: Proceedings of three state conferences*. San Francisco, CA: Far West Laboratories.

Busher, L. A. (1994). *The effects of peer coaching on elementary school teachers*. Paper presented at the annual meeting of the Eastern Educational Research Association, Sarasota, FL.

Caine, R. N., & Caine. G. (1997). *Education on the edge of possibility*. Alexandria, VA: Association for Supervision and Curriculum Development.

Carey, K. (2004). The real value of teachers: If good teachers matter, why don't we act like it? *Thinking K-16*, *8*(1), 3–43.

Cayuso, E., Fegan, C., & McAlister, D. (2013). *Designing teacher study groups: A guide for success*. New York, NY: Maupin.

Çimer, S., Çimer, S. O., & Vekli, G. S. (2013). How does reflection help teachers to become effective teachers? *International Journal of Educational Research*, *1*(4), 133–149.

Clotfelter, C. T., Ladd, H. F., & Vigdor, J. L. (2007). Teacher credentials and student achievement: Longitudinal analysis with student fixed effects. *Economics of Education Review*, *26*(6), 673–682.

Coburn, C. C., & Woulfin, S. L. (2012). Reading coaches and the relationship between policy and practice. *Reading Research Quarterly*, *47*(1), 5–30.

Cogan, M. (1973). *Clinical supervision*. Boston, MA: Houghton Mifflin Co.

Cosner, S. (2012). Leading the ongoing development of collaborative data practices. *Leadership and Policy in Schools*, *11*(1), 26–65.

Costa, A. L., & Garmston, R. J. ([1984]2002). *Cognitive coaching: A foundation for renaissance schools* (2nd ed.). Norwood, MA: Christopher-Gordon.

Daly, A. J. (2012). Data, dyads, and dynamics: Exploring data use and social networks in educational improvement. *Teachers College Record*, *114*(11), 1–38.

Darling-Hammond, L. (1999). *Teacher quality and student achievement: A review of state evidence*. Seattle, WA: Center for the Study of Teaching and Policy, University of Washington.

Darling-Hammond, L., & McLaughlin, M. W. (1995). Policies that support professional development in an era of reform. *Phi Delta Kappan, 76*, 597–604.

Darling-Hammond, L., Wei, C. R., Andree, A., Richardson, N, & Orphanos, S. (2009). *Professional learning in the learning profession: A status report on teacher development in the United States and abroad.* Oxford, OH: National Staff Development Council.

Denton, C. A., & Hasbrouck, J. A. N. (2009). A description of instructional coaching and its relationship to consultation. *Journal of Educational & Psychological Consultation, 19*, 150–175. doi: 10.1080/10474410802463296

Denton, C. A., Swanson, E. A., & Mathes, P. G. (2007). Assessment-based instructional coaching provided to reading intervention teachers. *Reading and Writing: An Interdisciplinary Journal, 20*, 569–590.

Deussen, T., Coskie, T., Robinson, L., & Autio, E. (2007). "Coach" can mean many things: Five categories of literacy coaches in Reading First (Issues & Answers Report, REL 2007-No. 005). Washington, DC: U.S. Department of Education, Institute of Education Sciences, National Center for Education Evaluation and Regional Assistance, Regional Educational Laboratory Northwest. Retrieved from http://ies.ed.gov/ncee/edlabs/regions/northwest/pdf/REL_2007005.pdf

Dole, J. A. (2004). The changing role of the reading specialist in school reform. *The Reading Teacher, 57*(5), 462–471.

Dunne, F., Evans, P., & Thompson-Grove, G. (n.d.). *Consultancy protocol.* Retrieved from http://schoolreforminitiative.org/doc/consultancy.pdf

Edwards, J. (2005). *Cognitive coaching research.* Highlands Ranch, CO: Center for Cognitive Coaching.

Ellison, J., & Hayes, C. (2009). Cognitive coaching. In J. Knight (Ed.), *Coaching: Approaches and perspectives* (pp. 70–90). Thousand Oaks, CA: Corwin.

Elmore, R. (2004). *School reform from the inside out.* Cambridge, MA: Harvard University Press.

Elmore, R. F., & Burney, D. (1998). Improving instruction through professional development in New York City's community district #2. *CPRE Policy Bulletin.* Retrieved from www.cpre.org/sites/default/files/policybulletin/901_pb-02.pdf

Fredricks, J., Blumenfeld, P., & Paris, A. (2004). School engagement: Potential of the concept, state of the evidence. *American Education Research Association, 74*(1), 59–109. Retrieved from http://ceep.indiana.edu/hssse/Fredricks.pdf

Fullan, M. (2001). *Leading in a culture of change.* San Francisco, CA: Jossey-Bass

Fullan, M., & Knight, J. (2011). Coaches as system leaders. *Educational Leadership, 69*(2), 50–53.

Garmston, R., Linder, C., & Whitaker, J. (1993). Reflections on cognitive coaching. *Educational Leadership, 51*(2), 57–61.

Gersten R., Dimino J., Jayanthi M., Kim J. S., & Santoro, L.E. (2010). Teacher study group: Impact of the professional development model on reading instruction and student outcomes in first grade classrooms. *American Educational Research Journal, 47*(3), 694–739.

Gibson, S. A. (2006). Lesson observation and feedback: The practice of an expert reading coach. *Reading Research & Instruction, 45*(4), 295–318.

Goe, L., & Stickler, L. M. (2008). *Teacher quality and student achievement: Making the most of recent research*. Washington, DC: National Comprehensive Center for Teacher Quality. Retrieved from http://files.eric.ed.gov/fulltext/ED520769.pdf

Goldhammer, R. (1969). *Clinical supervision*. New York, NY: Holt, Rinehart, & Winston.

Goodwin, B., & Hein, H. (2016). Research says: Looking at student work yields insights. *Educational Leadership, 73*(7), 79–80.

Grimm, E. D., Kaufman, T., & Doty, D. (2014). Rethinking classroom observation. *Educational Leadership, 71*(8), 24–29.

Gross, P. A. (2010). Not another trend. Secondary-level literacy coaching. *The Clearing House: A Journal of Educational Strategies, Issues and Ideas, 83*(4), 133–137.

Gulamhussein, A. (2013). *Teaching the teachers. Effective professional development in an era of high stakes accountability*. The Center for Public Education. Retrieved from www.centerforpubliceducation.org/Main-Menu/Staffingstudents/Teaching-the-Teachers-Effective-Professional-Development-in-an-Era-of-High-Stakes-Accountability/Teaching-the-Teachers-Full-Report.pdf

Guskey, T. R., & Sparks, D. (1991). What to consider when evaluating staff development. *Educational Leadership, 49*(3), 73–76.

Hamilton, L., Halverson, R., Jackson, S., Mandinach, E., Supovitz, J., & Wayman, J. (2009). *Using student achievement data to support instructional decision making* (NCEE 2009-4067). Washington, DC: National Center for Education Evaluation and Regional Assistance, Institute of Education Sciences, U.S. Department of Education. Retrieved from http://ies.ed.gov/ncee/wwc/publications/practice guides/

Hanford, E. (2015, August 27). *A different approach to teacher learning: Lesson study*. Retrieved from www.americanradioworks.org/segments/a-different-approach-to-teacher-learning-lesson-study/

Hanover Research. (2014). *Best practices in instructional coaching*. Retrieved from http://ciscsymposium.sccoe.org/wp-content/uploads/2016/02/Best-Practices-in-Instructional-Coaching.pdf

Harrington, H. J., Voehl, F., & Voehl, C. F. (2014). *Model for sustainable change* [White paper]. Retrieved from www.pmi.org

Hasbrouck, J. & Denton, C. (2005). *The reading coach: A how-to manual for success*. Boston, MA: Sopris West.

Hattie, J. A. (1992). Measuring the effects of schooling. *Australian Journal of Education*, *36*(1), 5–13.

Hattie, J., & Timperley, H. (2007). The power of feedback. *Review of Educational Research*, *77*(1), 81–112. doi: 10.3102/003465430298487

Hawley, W. D., & Valli, L. (1999). The essentials of effective professional development: A new consensus. In L. Darling-Hammond & G. Sykes (Eds.), *Teaching as a learning profession* (pp. 127–150). San Francisco, CA: Jossey-Bass.

Heineke, S. F. (2010). Reading coaching discourse: Practical applications. In J. Cassidy, S. Garrett, & M. Sailors (Eds.), *Literacy coaching: Research and practice*. Corpus Christi, TX: Consortium for Educational Development, Evaluation, and Research, Texas A&M University-Corpus Christi.

Herman, J. L., Yamashiro, K., Lefkowitz, S., & Trusela, L. A. (2008). *Exploring data use and school performance in an urban public school district: Evaluation of Seattle Public Schools' comprehensive value-added system* (CRESST Report 742). Los Angeles, CA: National Center for Research on Evaluation, Standards, and Student Testing. Retrieved from www.cse.ucla.edu/products/reports/R742.pdf

Hightower, A. M., Delgado, R. C., Lloyd, S. C., Wittenstein, R., Sellers, K., & Swanson, C. B. (2011). *Improving student learning by supporting quality teaching: Key issues, effective strategies*. Bethesda, MD: Editorial Projects in Education, Inc. Retrieved from www.edweek.org/media/eperc_qualityteaching_12.11.pdf

Honey, P., & Mumford, A. (1982) *Manual of learning styles*. London, UK: P Honey.

Hurd, J., & Lewis, C. (2011). *Lesson study step by step: How teacher learning communities improve instruction*. Portsmouth, NH: Heinemann.

International Reading Association. (2010). *Standards for reading professionals—revised 2010*. Newark, DE: Author.

Johnson, A., Checkley, J., & Baker, R. (2006). *Getting results with curriculum mapping: Facilitator's guide*. Alexandria, VA: ASCD.

Jordan, H. R., Mendro, R. L., & Weerasinghe, D. (1997, July 16). *Teacher effects on longitudinal student achievement: A report on research in progress*. Paper presented at annual meeting of CREATE, Indianapolis, IN.

Joyce, B., Bush, R., & McKibbin, M. (1982). *The California staff development study. The January 1982 report*. Palo Alto, CA: Booksend Laboratories.

Joyce, B., & Showers, B. (1980). Improving inservice training: The messages of research. *Educational Leadership*, *37*(5), 379–385.

Joyce, B., & Showers, B. (1996). The evolution of peer coaching. *Educational Leadership*, *53*(6), 12–16.

Joyce, B., & Showers, B. (2002). *Student achievement through staff development*. Alexandria, VA: ASCD.

Kane, T. (2012, Fall). Capturing the dimensions of effective teaching. *Education Next*, 35–41.

Kessler, A. M., Stein, M. K., & Schunn, C. D. (2015). Cognitive demand of model tracing tutor tasks: Conceptualizing and predicting how deeply students engage. *Tech Know Learn.* doi: 10.1007/s10758-015-9248-6. Retrieved from www.lrdc.pitt.edu/schunn/research/papers/kessler-stein-schunn2015.pdf

Killion, J. (2008). Coaches help mine the data. *Teachers Teaching Teachers, 3*(5), 7–8.

Killion, J. (2009). Coaches' roles, responsibilities, and reach. In J. Knight (Ed.), *Coaching: Approaches and perspectives* (pp. 7–28). Thousand Oaks, CA: Corwin.

Knight, J. (2000). *Another damn thing we've got to do: Teacher perceptions of professional development.* Paper presented at the meeting of the American Educational Research Association, New Orleans, LA.

Knight, J. (2004). Progress through partnership. *Journal of Staff Development, 25*(2), 32–37.

Knight, J. (2005). A primer on instructional coaches. *Principal Leadership, 5*(9), 16–21.

Knight, J. (2006). Instructional coaching: Eight factors for realizing better classroom teaching through support, feedback and intensive, individualized professional learning. *The School Administrator, 63*(4), 36–40.

Knight, J. (2007). *Instructional coaching: A partnership approach to improving instruction.* Thousand Oaks, CA: Corwin.

Knight, J. (2009a). Instructional coaching. In J. Knight (Ed.), *Coaching: Approaches and perspectives* (pp. 29–55). Thousand Oaks, CA: Corwin.

Knight, J. (2009b). What can we do about teacher resistance? *Phi Delta Kappan, 90*(7), 508–513.

Knight, J., Elford, M., Hock, M., Dunekack, D., Bradley, B., Deshler, D. D., & Knight, D. (2015). 3 steps to great coaching: A simple but powerful instructional coaching cycle nets results. *Journal of Staff Development, 36*(1), 10–18.

Knowles, M. (1980). The *modern practice of adult education: From pedagogy to andragogy.* Englewoods Cliff, NJ: Cambridge Adult Education.

Knowles, M. (1984a). *The adult learner: A neglected species* (3rd ed.). Houston, TX: Gulf Publishing.

Knowles, M. (1984b). *Andragogy in action.* San Francisco, CA: Jossey-Bass.

Knowles, M. S., Holton III, E. F., & Swanson, R. A. (1998.) *The adult learner: The definitive classic in adult education and human resource development* (5th ed.). Houston, TX: Gulf Publishing Company.

Kolb, D. A. (1984). *Experiential learning: Experience as the source of learning and development.* Englewood Cliffs, NJ: Prentice-Hall, Inc.

L'Allier, S.K., & Elish-Piper, L. (2006, December). *An initial examination of the effects of literacy coaching on student achievement in reading in grades K-3.* Paper presented at the annual conference of the National Reading Conference, Los Angeles, CA.

L'Allier, S., Elish-Piper, L., & Bean, R. M. (2010). What matters for elementary literacy coaching? Guiding principles for instructional improvement and student achievement. *Reading Teacher, 63*(7), 544–554.

Lewis, C. (2000, April). Lesson study: The core of Japanese professional development. Paper presented at the annual meeting of the American Educational Research Association, New Orleans, LA.

Lewis, C., Perry, R., & Friedkin, S. (2009). Lesson study as action research. In S. E. Noffke & B. Somekh (Eds.), *The Sage handbook of educational action research* (pp. 142–154). Thousand Oaks, CA: SAGE.

Lewis, C. C., & Hurd, J. (2011). *Lesson study step by step: How teacher learning communities improve instruction.* Portsmouth, NH: Heinemann.

Lieberman, A. (1995). Practices that support teacher development: *Transforming conceptions of professional learning. Innovating and evaluating science education: NSF evaluation forums, 1992–94.* Retrieved from www.nsf.gov/pubs/1995/nsf95162/nsf_ef.pdf

Literacy Collaborative. (2009). *The positive effects of literacy collaborative on teaching and student learning: A federally funded value-added study.* Retrieved from www.literacycollaborative.org/docs/TQ-summary-for-website-new.pdf

Lopez, S. J., & Calderon, V. (2011). Gallup student poll: Measuring and promoting, what is right with students. *Applied Positive Psychology: Improving Everyday Life, Schools, Work, Health, and Society,* 117–134.

Marsh, J. A., McCombs, J. S., & Martorell, F. (2012). Reading coach quality: Findings from Florida middle schools. *Literacy Research and Instruction, 51*(1), 1–26.

Marsh, J. A., McCombs, J. S., & Naftel, S. (2008, March). *Building teacher capacity through literacy coaching: Findings from the Florida middle school study.* Paper presented at the annual meeting of the American Educational Research Association, New York, NY.

Matsumura, L. C., Garnier, H. E., & Resnick, L. B. (2010). Implementing literacy coaching: The role of school social resources. *Educational Evaluation and Policy Analysis, 32*(2), 249–272.

Means, B., Chen, E., DeBarger, A., & Padilla, C. (2011). *Teachers' ability to use data to inform instruction: Challenges and supports.* Washington, DC: U. S. Department of Education, Office of Planning, Evaluation and Policy Development.

Mizell, H. (2010). *Why professional development matters.* Retrieved from https://learning forward.org/docs/pdf/why_pd_matters_web.pdf?sfvrsn=0

Murphy, C. (1992). Study groups foster schoolwide learning. *Educational Leadership, 50*(3), 71–74.

NASBE. (2015). *A State of Engagement: NASBE Study Group on Student Engagement.* Retrieved from www.nasbe.org/wp-content/uploads/StudentEngagement StudyGroupReport_March-2015_FINAL1.pdf

National Staff Development Council. (n.d.). *Peer coaching.* Retrieved from www.polk-fl.net/staff/professionaldevelopment/documents/Chapter16-Peer Coaching.pdf

National School Reform Faculty. (n.d.). *Consultancy: Adapted for examining student work.* Retrieved from www.nsrfharmony.org/system/files/protocols/consult_stud_work_0.pdf

Neufeld, B., & Roper, D. (2003). *Coaching: A strategy for developing instructional capacity: Promises and practicalities.* Washington, DC: Aspen Institute Program on Education and Annenberg Institute for School Reform. Retrieved from http://annenberginstitute.org/pdf/Coaching.pdf

Neumerski, C. (2013). Rethinking instructional leadership, a review: What do we know about principal, teacher, and coach instructional leadership and where should we go from here? *Educational Administration Quarterly, 49*(2), 310–347.

Nye, B., Konstantopoulos, S., & Hedges, L. V. (2004). How large are teacher effects? *Educational Evaluation and Policy Analysis, 26,* 237–257.

Oláh, L. N., Lawrence, N. R., & Riggan, M. (2010). Learning to learn from benchmark assessment data: How teachers analyze results. *Peabody Journal of Education, 85*(1), 226–245.

Opfer, V. D., & Pedder, D. (2011). Conceptualizing teacher professional learning. *Review of Educational Research, 81,* 376–407. doi: 10.3102/0034654311413609

Perkins, S. J. (1988). On becoming a peer coach: Practices, identities, and beliefs of inexperienced coaches. *Journal of Curriculum and Supervision, 13*(3), 235–254.

Perry, A. (2011). Teacher preparation programs: A critical vehicle to drive student achievement. *Re:Vision, 1,* 1–8.

Porter, A. C., & Smithson, J. L. (2001). *Defining, developing, and using curriculum indicators.* CPRE Research Reports. Retrieved from http://repository.upenn.edu/cpre_researchreports/69

Puig, E. A., & Froelich, K. S. (2007). *The literacy coach: Guiding in the right direction.* Boston, MA: Allyn & Bacon/Pearson.

Resnick, L. B., & Hall, M. W. (2000). *Principles of learning for effort-based education.* Pittsburgh, PA: University of Pittsburgh.

Rice, J. K. (2003). *Teacher quality: Understanding the effectiveness of teacher attributes.* Retrieved from www.epi.org/publication/books_teacher_quality_execsum_intro/

Robbins, P. (2015). *Peer coaching to enrich professional practice, school culture, and student learning.* Alexandria, VA: ASCD.

Rowan, B., Correnti, R., & Miller, R. J. (2002). *What large-scale survey research tells us about teacher effects on student achievement: Insights from the prospects study of elementary schools.* (CPRE Research Report Series RR-051). Philadelphia, PA: Consortium for Policy Research in Education.

Sanders, W., & Rivers, J. (1996). *Cumulative and residual effects of teachers on future student academic achievement.* Knoxville, TN: University of Tennessee Value-Added Research and Assessment Center.

Saphier, J., & West, L. (2009/2010). How coaches can maximize student learning. *Phi Delta Kappan*, *91*(4), 46–50.

Showers, B., & Joyce, B. (1996). The evolution of peer coaching. *Educational Leadership*, *53*(6), 12–16.

Stahl, S. A., & Heubach, K. M. (2005). Fluency-oriented reading instruction. *Journal of Literacy Research*, *37*, 25–60.

Stover, K., Kissel, B., Haag, K., & Shoniker, R. (2011). Differentiated coaching: Fostering reflection with teachers. *The Reading Teacher*, *64*(7), 498–509. doi: 10.1598/ RT.64.7.3

Strong, M., Fletcher, S., & Villar, A. (2004). *An investigation of the effects of teacher experience and teacher preparedness on the performance of Latino students in California.* Santa Cruz, CA: New Teacher Center.

Sugai, G. (1983). Making a teacher study group work. *Teacher Education and Special Education*, *6*, 173–178.

Swanson, K., Allen, G., & Mancabelli, R. (2016). Eliminating the blame game. *Educational Leadership*, *73*(3), 68–71.

Sykes, G. (1999). Teacher and student learning. In L. Darling-Hammond & G. Sykes (Eds.), *Teaching as a learning profession* (pp. 151–179). San Francisco, CA: Jossey-Bass.

Taylor, B., & Kroth, M. (2009). Andragogy's transition into The future: Meta-analysis of andragogy and its search for a measurable instrument. *Journal of Adult Education*, *38*(1), 1–11.

Toll, C. A. (2009). Literacy coaching. In J. Night (Ed.), *Coaching approaches and perspectives* (pp. 56–69). Thousand Oaks, CA: Corwin Press.

Toll, C. A. (2014). *The literacy coach's survival guide: Essential questions and practical answers.* Newark, DE: International Reading Association.

Tomlinson, C. A. (2000, August). *Differentiation of instruction in the elementary grades.* ERIC Digest. ERIC Clearinghouse on Elementary and Early Childhood Education.

Trotter, Y. D. (2006). Adult learning theories: Impacting professional development programs. *The Delta Kappa Gamma Bulletin*, *72*(2), 8–13.

Tschannen-Moran, B., & Tschannen-Moran, M. (2010). *Evocative coaching.* San Francisco, CA: Jossey-Bass.

U. S. Department of Education. (2009). *Implementing data-informed decision making in schools: Teacher access, supports and use.* Washington, DC: U. S. Department of Education, Office of Planning, Evaluation and Policy Development.

U. S. Department of Education. (2010). *Use of education data at the local level from accountability to instructional improvement.* Washington, DC: U.S. Department of Education, Office of Planning, Evaluation and Policy Development.

Vygotsky, L. S. (1978). *Mind in society: The development of higher psychological processes.* Cambridge, MA: Harvard University Press.

Walpole, S., & Blamey, K. L. (2008). Elementary literacy coaches: The reality of dual roles. *The Reading Teacher, 62*(3), 222–231.

Wayman, J. C., Cho, V., & Johnston, M. T. (2007). *The data-informed district: A district-wide evaluation of data use in the Natrona County School District.* Austin, TX: University of Texas.

West, L. (2009). Content coaching: Transforming the teaching profession. In J. Knight (Ed.), *Coaching: Approaches and perspectives* (pp. 29–55). Thousand Oaks, CA: Corwin.

West, L., & Cameron, A. (2013). *Agents of change: How content coaching transforms teaching & learning.* Portsmouth: NH: Heinemann.

Whitney, A., Blau, S., Bright, A., Cabe, R., Dewar, T., Levin, J., Macias, R., & Rogers, P. (2008). Beyond strategies: Teacher practice, writing process, and the influence of inquiry. *English Education, 40*(3), 201–230. Retrieved from www.nwp.org/cs/public/

Windschitl, M., Thompson, J., & Braaten, M. (2011). Ambitious pedagogy by novice teachers? Who benefits from tool-supported collaborative inquiry into practice and why. *Teachers College Record, 113*(7), 1311–1360.

Wren, S. (2005). Literacy coaches: Promises and problems. Paper presented at the annual meeting of the National Reading Conference, Miami, FL.

Wright, S. P., Horn, S. P., & Sanders, W. L. (1997). Teacher and classroom context effects on student achievement: Implications for teacher evaluation. *Journal of Personnel Evaluation in Education, 11*(1), 57–67.

Yoon, K. S., Duncan, T., Lee, S. W. Y., Scarloss, B., & Shapley, K. (2007). *Reviewing the evidence on how teacher professional development affects student achievement.* (Issues & Answer Report, REL 2007-No. 033) Washington, DC: U. S. Department of Education, Institute of Education Sciences, National Center for Education Evaluation and Regional Assistance, Regional Educational Laboratory Southwest. Retrieved from http://ies.ed.gov/ncec/edlabs

Appendix A
Coaching Moves Rating Scale

Determine how frequently you engage in the following professional practices within each literacy coach role. Identifying the rate of occurrence will allow you to detect in what roles you devote most of your energies as well as roles that you may be inadvertently neglecting, which will ensure that you broaden your work and the effect that you have in your school.

Literacy Coach Role	Professional Practices	Frequency of Occurrence		
		Never (0 times a month)	Sometimes (2–4 times a month)	Frequently (5 times or more a month)
Change Agent	◆ Collaborate with administrators to define vision for school improvement ◆ Work with administrators to set focused, prescriptive professional development goals to plan for school improvement ◆ View all responsibilities and tasks through the lens of a change agent ◆ Maintain solution-driven focus ◆ Lead inquiry into best practices ◆ Collaborate with all teachers; don't become a "fixer" of underperforming teachers ◆ Model evidence-based teaching ◆ Advocate for student learning ◆ Facilitate continuous improvement ◆ Be patient but persistent			

Literacy Coach Role	Professional Practices	Frequency of Occurrence		
		Never (0 times a month)	Sometimes (2–4 times a month)	Frequently (5 times or more a month)
Relationship Builder	◆ Foster a safe environment ◆ Develop collegial relationships ◆ Listen ◆ Maintain confidentiality ◆ Follow through on requests ◆ Seek out teachers for professional dialogue ◆ Understand that coaching is not a top down model ◆ Set clear expectations for work between the coach and the classroom teacher ◆ Link coaching model to the needs of individual teachers ◆ End the misconception that coaching operates as a deficit model for only those teachers who need to be "fixed" ◆ Welcome teachers' initiation of coaching support ◆ Support teacher experimentation with new practices ◆ Ask open-ended questions to spur deeper thinking ◆ Encourage self-reflection of professional practices			
Data Analyst	◆ Offer demonstrations of assessment administration and scoring to ensure a standardized approach to grading practices ◆ Collaborate with teachers to analyze and interpret data ◆ Identify teacher needs based on data ◆ Support teachers in their ability to use data to drive instruction ◆ Emphasize a problem-solving lens			

	◆ Rely on student data to ground coaching support ◆ Help teachers adjust instructional strategies based on data and student need ◆ Guide teachers in their monitoring of student data			
Curriculum Expert	◆ Demonstrate thorough knowledge of current research and pedagogy ◆ Dissect standards for better understanding of key knowledge, skills, and learning outcomes ◆ Focus coaching on content-specific standards ◆ Guide teachers in understanding curriculum ◆ Augment teacher content knowledge ◆ Support teachers in implementing curriculum ◆ Define and make transparent the different curriculum types ◆ Assist teachers in delivering the core curriculum ◆ Collaborate on assessments that measure student learning of curriculum			
Resource Manager	◆ Demonstrate knowledge of where to locate appropriate resources for classroom instruction and improving teacher practice ◆ Seek out resources that will benefit the school, individual classrooms, and the differentiated needs of students ◆ Locate and provide instructional materials requested by teachers ◆ Share research and best practices ◆ Expand the repertoire of instructional resources utilized by teachers			

Literacy Coach Role	Professional Practices	Frequency of Occurrence		
		Never (0 times a month)	Sometimes (2–4 times a month)	Frequently (5 times or more a month)
Instructional Specialist	◆ Demonstrate comprehensive knowledge of evidence-based practices ◆ Use assessment to drive coaching and instruction ◆ Observe and provide feedback based on measurable objectives ◆ Collaborate in planning and delivery of lessons (short-term objectives) and units (long-range goals) ◆ Model well-designed lessons ◆ Aid teachers in forming instructional groups ◆ Suggest appropriate differentiated practices ◆ Stay abreast of technology ◆ Pose questions that elicit reflection and is solution-driven ◆ Focus on using assessment for learning			
Professional Developer	◆ Understand adult learning theory ◆ Administer professional development needs survey ◆ Nurture a culture of professional inquiry ◆ Develop professional development plan based on evidence-based needs of students and teachers ◆ Offer a range of professional development opportunities, e.g., faculty workshop, teacher study group, lesson study, coaching cycles suited to student learning needs, coaching goals, and individual teacher practice ◆ Engage in coaching rotations that include coaching cycles (for all teachers) as well as consultancies (both teacher-driven and administrative referrals)			

Appendix B
Professional Developer Resources

TABLE 9.3 Elementary School Needs Survey

Please note the three topics that would most enhance your instructional skills. They may include a literacy focus, content area study, or instructional strategies.

Reading

___ Phonological awareness

___ Decoding skills

___ Morphology (prefixes, roots, and suffixes)

___ Vocabulary development

___ Comprehensive strategies

Writing

___ Building sentences

___ Constructing paragraphs

___ Grammar and mechanics

___ Narrative writing

___ Informative/explanatory writing

___ Opinion writing

Speaking & Listening

___ Collaborative discussions

___ Active listening

___ Student presentations

Instructional Planning

___ Using data to drive instruction

___ Lesson planning

___ Unit planning

___ Student engagement

___ Crafting instruction

Building an Instructional Repertoire

___ Differentiation

___ Critical thinking

___ Instructional rigor

___ Classroom management

___ Struggling learners

___ English language learners

Content Area Study

___ Content area reading

___ Taking notes

___ Study Skills

TABLE 9.4 Secondary School Needs Survey

Please check which areas of professional development are your priority for instructional improvement during the upcoming academic year.

Interactive Learning Strategies	Best Practices
___ Pre-Reading	___ Student Engagement
___ During Reading	___ Classroom Management
___ Post-Reading	___ Critical Thinking
___ Vocabulary	___ Academic Rigor
___ Writing Across the Disciplines	___ Differentiation

Diverse Learners	Assessment
___ At-Risk Students	___ Authentic Assessment Tools
___ Struggling Readers	___ Developing Student Rubrics
___ Students with Special Needs	___ Constructing Quality Assessments
___ Disengaged Learners	___ Interpreting Assessment Results
___ English Language Learners	___ Data-Driven Instruction

TABLE 9.5 Planning Worksheet for Modeling in the Classroom

Modeling Objective _____

Modeled Lesson/Strategy _____

Guiding Questions

◆ What will the teacher be doing while the lesson /strategy is being modeled (e.g., scripting, taking notes, tracking student behaviors)?

◆ What will the teacher be able to do after observing this lesson/strategy?

◆ In what ways will modeling influence student learning?

◆ How will professional learning be sustained after modeling (e.g., professional dialogue, co-planning, teacher observation and feedback loop)?

TABLE 9.6 LASW Guided Analysis and Reflection

Before Reviewing Student Work	While Reviewing Student Work	After Reviewing Student Work
◆ What standard is being addressed in this work sample? ◆ Where does this work sample fall within the instructional sequence? What has already been taught? What will be taught after this work sample? ◆ What is deemed "proficient" for this work? Did the student(s) know these expectations? ◆ How long did the student(s) work on this assignment?	◆ How does this work meet/ not meet the standards? ◆ What does this work tell us about what the student(s) understands? ◆ What strengths does the work demonstrate? ◆ What deficits does the work show? ◆ Do any patterns emerge about student thinking and learning? ◆ What instruction might support students from the point they are currently?	◆ What did you discover about student learning based on this process? ◆ What insights did you gain from your colleagues? ◆ Did you see or hear anything today that was surprising or intriguing? ◆ How might you adjust your instruction in reaction to what you learned today? ◆ Did this process raise any questions about teaching and learning for you?

TABLE 9.7 Pre-Conferencing Planning Sheet

Pre-Conference Planning Sheet	
Teacher's Name: Grade Level: Content Area:	Length of Coaching Cycle:
Student-Learning Goal:	Notes:
Coaching Goal:	Notes:
Scheduling for Classroom Visits:	Scheduling for Debriefs:
Literacy Coach Responsibilities:	Classroom Teacher Responsibilities:
Student Work Products/Assessments to Be Collected as Evidence of Effective Practice:	
Confirming Evidence That Coaching Cycle Has Reached Its Goal:	

TABLE 9.8 Observational Notes

Observational Notes	
Instructor's Name:	Date:
Coaching Goal:	Lesson Focus:
What the Instructor Said:	What the Instructor Did:
How the Students Responded:	Evidence of Student Learning:
Additional Notes:	

TABLE 9.9 Post-Conference Recording Form

Post-Conference Recording Form	
Teacher Name: Grade/Content Area: Date:	
Lesson Focus:	*How did the lesson go? Were students successful? Based on what evidence?*
Student Learning Goal:	*Was the goal met? Based on what evidence?*
Coaching Goal:	*Was the goal met? Based on what evidence?*
What are your next steps?	*How can I support you?*
Additional Notes:	

TABLE 9.10 Coaching Planning Worksheet

Teacher's Name: Grade Level: Content Area:	Length of Coaching Cycle:
Student-Learning Goal:	Notes:
Coaching Goal:	Notes:

Coaching Support: Identify the role(s) needed to offer support and how collaboration will take place.

Data Analyst	Resource Manager	Curriculum Expert	Instructional Specialist	Professional Developer

If professional development is selected, check the form(s) of professional development to be implemented. ◆ Faculty Workshop ◆ Team Meeting ◆ Classroom Visitation ◆ Teacher Study Group ◆ Observation & Feedback Loop ◆ Modeling ◆ Co-Planning ◆ Co-Teaching ◆ Lesson Study ◆ Looking at Student Work ◆ Examining Achievement Data ◆ Coaching Cycle	Notes:
Student Work Products/Assessments to Be Collected:	Notes:

Confirming Evidence That Coaching Goal Has Been Met:

TABLE 10.1 Reflective Practice After a Coaching Rotation

Coaching Process	Guiding Questions for Literacy Coach	Responses
Goals & Objectives	◆ What instructional goal was set for this coaching rotation? ◆ What learning objective was identified for this coaching rotation?	
Actions	◆ In attempting to reach your goal/objective, what went well? ◆ How do you know? ◆ Can you replicate that success with other coaching rotations? ◆ In attempting to reach your goal/objective, what didn't go as well? ◆ How do you know? ◆ What can you change for future coaching rotations?	
Outcomes	◆ Did you reach your goal/objective? ◆ How do you know?	
Feedback	◆ What feedback did you receive from your classroom colleague?	

What have you learned from this process and what aspects of your coaching will you change to improve your practice?

Appendix C
Professional Book Club—Questions for Study and Reflection

PART I: How Important Is Coaching for Teaching and Learning?

1. Do you agree with Joyce and Showers that teachers need 20–25 trials in a classroom before new learning becomes cemented in teacher practice? Why or why not?
2. Does the traditional one-time professional development session have any merit for professional learning?

Chapter 1: The Evolution of Coaching as a Professional Development Model
1. Set a timer. In 1 minute or less, explain coaching as a professional development model and the value it holds for enhancing teacher practice and student learning outcomes.
   - Is it fair to task literacy coaches with being responsible for school reform?
   - What would you include in the job description for a literacy coach? How does it align with what we know about effective professional learning?

Chapter 2: Models of Coaching
1. Think back to a classroom teacher with whom you have worked. Did your efforts fit within one or more of the coaching models? How so? Were your efforts effective?
2. Which model of coaching (i.e., peer, cognitive, instructional, content) do you gravitate toward the most? Why?
3. How important do you believe formal training in coaching models is to the ultimate success of a literacy coach?

PART II: What Roles Does a Literacy Coach Play?

1. What does a typical day look like in a literacy coach's life? How many of the tasks link to teacher practice?
2. Describe what a "perfect" coaching day would look like.

Chapter 3: Change Agent

1. In thinking of yourself as a change agent, what do you believe is the most significant area for change in your school? Why?
2. Devise a list of steps that would support and sustain such a change. Why did you choose the items that you did?
3. Do you as a literacy coach need any tools to support this change (e.g., professional development for yourself, further research, instructional resources, financial resources, human resources)?

Chapter 4: Relationship Builder

1. How do you build a strong partnership with your administrator?
2. Describe a coaching relationship you've had. How did you initiate the relationship?
3. What do you believe makes a literacy coach–classroom teacher relationship successful?

Chapter 5: Data Analyst

1. Select one student in your school to be a candidate for you to follow through the Student Data Loop. Describe the outcome of each step.
2. Choose a piece of student work and conduct a scoring party with your colleagues. What were the results?
3. Within your school system, what do you believe are the three most significant pieces of student data that should be examined and analyzed? Why did you select them? In what ways are they more important than other data points?

Chapter 6: Curriculum Expert

1. What is your stance on the literacy coach as learner or expert? Is it one or the other? A combination of the two? Why?
2. How do you guide your classroom colleagues in their understanding of curriculum?
3. Does your core district/school curriculum (curriculum scope and sequence, curriculum map, pacing guide, anthologies, instructional materials) align to the intended curriculum (state standards) and assessed curriculum (state, district, and school assessments). If not, where is the disconnect?

Chapter 7: Resource Manager

1. How do you determine what resources your school needs?
2. What do you believe every school should have in the way of resources?
3. What is the effect of resources on student learning in your school?

Chapter 8: Instructional Specialist

1. What do you define as "best practice" in literacy instruction?
2. Think back to a time when you collaborated with a classroom colleague on cognitively demanding instruction. What did that look like?
3. In what ways do you help classroom colleagues differentiate their instructional practice and learning opportunities for students?

Chapter 9: Professional Developer

1. Which aspect of the adult learning theories discussed in this chapter do you believe is the most significant in planning and implementing professional development? Why?
2. For personal reflection (not group discussion), consider the following questions. What kind of professional developer am I? What are my strengths? In what ways can I improve?
3. During the last academic year, which of the 12 forms of professional development discussed in this chapter have you implemented the most? What informed your decision to use this type of professional development? Was it effective? Why?

PART III: How Does a Coach Ensure Lasting Change?

1. Share one area of your school's vision that you consider sustainable through a professional development plan and student data monitoring. How will these elements support long-term change?
2. Describe what modes of communication you would utilize to sustain change.

Chapter 10: Self-Reflection and Sustaining Change

1. How often do you self-reflect about your own practice? Has it changed your practice? If yes, in what ways? If no, why not?
2. How would you determine if you had a successful coaching year? What does success look like?
3. In what ways do you think you can sustain momentum in ensuring lasting change?